D1630350

The World
is
My Mirror

Richard Bates

NON-DUALITY PRESS

THE WORLD IS MY MIRROR

First edition published September 2012 by NON-DUALITY PRESS

© Richard Bates 2012
© Non-Duality Press 2012

Illustration (p.iv) by Edward Ballard

Richard Bates has asserted his right under the Copyright, Designs
and Patents Act, 1988, to be identified as author of this work.

NON-DUALITY PRESS | PO Box 2228 | Salisbury | SP2 2GZ
United Kingdom

ISBN: 978-1-908664-26-6

www.non-dualitypress.org

Dedication

This book has appeared because I crossed paths with one very special person.

Many people who write about the unfathomable and mysterious phenomenon we call life or existence seem to have had a number of years reading spiritual books and quite a few trips to exotic places to hear the words of the enlightened. For me, there was none of this.

I was a tough-minded individual that was just plain anxious and unhappy. I knew what I knew, and that was that.

Lynn 'Foxy', you were my guru who I never even searched for. You appeared when it was time for you to appear and to kick-start a journey I never knew I needed.

Your cosmic energy and aliveness broke through the toughest skin of any human.

This book is dedicated to you, Lynn.

iv

The Game

Furrowed brow
To furrowed frown
I'll choose my move
I'll usurp your crown

All is set
Let the games commence
Check the rules
And make it tense

The appearance of heat
The first glimpse of fire
Look at me now
Let our faces retire

Touch my hand
Let's embrace our demise
The flames of collapse
Enlighten the wise

The ash of destruction
It's over too soon
The tick of a clock
A finger to the moon

Awaken my friend
It's all been a game
It's fun to get caught
But it ends all the same

Contents

Setting the Scene

Here we are, you and I, sitting in a little country pub somewhere in the thick of winter, by the inglenook fireplace. We are watching the flames licking up the chimney as we see the snow flurries out of the window. Dusk approaches. There's the satisfying comfort that I have booked an overnight stay and the barman goes to bed only when I have downed my last pint of real ale, brewed locally and tasting like nectar. We contemplate how far we have come in this crazy life and where it is all leading to. We relax back in our red leather armchairs, pick at our snack of strong cheese and fresh crusty bread, whilst we just talk and ponder. Come and join me in the pages of this book.

So what is this book all about? Does the world really need another book about non-duality? What can this one say that other books cannot?

What follows is an ordinary bloke's description of this amazing, unfathomable thing called Wholeness, oneness, and liberation. I want to convey that liberation is not somewhere else and at some other time. It is here in the everyday life that is totally fresh and totally new. I have not referred to many teachers and have not placed poems or aphorisms at the beginning of every chapter.

To anyone flicking through this to see what all the fuss is about and with no real interest, I apologise. Prior to 2008, I would have been with you and put the book down again. I have no answer why this gripped me at the time it did. All I know is it just happens, like the heart beating and the food digesting. It seems life can be confused and life can be clear. But I will say this: there is an energy here that is totally ruthless and will stop at nothing until it finds. This unseen leviathan makes infinity look small. The frustration is that if you find yourself seeking and discover this kind of message it can drive you nuts because what you think you are seeking for will not succumb to pressure. I cannot give you what you seek because you do not have anything more or less than I do. Seeking and not finding, believe it or not, is not so bad. When not finding is finding, where do you go and where have you been? What follows is the best I can do, now.

You will have to see for yourself what this is about. You have to taste the food before you leave the restaurant; if you eat the menu it's a bit cardboardy and stale. What I try to do is to use what we have to hand, to explore experience — not to eliminate it.

The message of this book is that what appears to happen, does not. To see this may require investigation on a grand scale. Use the mind and take it to its limits. If you feel like a doer, then 'do'. You do not need to listen to those teachings which go for the jugular and say there is no you that can neither do or not do. I am not saying that it's an incorrect formulation — it is not. The thing is when 'you' can say that, knowing it comes from a place you never thought existed, your disappearance will be your everything. The teachings and the teachers are like a boat that carries you across the river; they are left for someone else to use going another way. I wonder if that could be called compassion?

I suggested that you 'use the mind' and the mind is an awesome piece of kit, but it can take on too much too easily. Asking it to contemplate consciousness, awareness or no-thingness will cause it to malfunction. The mind's a very practical fellow and can come up with some useful strategies to keep this body functioning and life happening: it adapts in milliseconds, not millennia. Take, for example, the ability to recognise a familiar face among crowds of thousand: quite a feat if you bear in mind faces do not differ in the same way a tree differs from a sausage.

So the mind deserves respect. It does its job admirably. It creates colour, sound and furnishes a world for you with interesting things to entertain and excite you. But why not respect its limits? Give it some space now and again and allow it to rest. I promise it will thank you.

The mind is a label slapper: drawing lines and making things appear to be solid and unchanging. It loves to predict and to know. This is a survival strategy that has great benefit to this sophisticated tube that puts things in one end and expels from the other. The mind and body function perfectly in the environment that created them.

The mind is also soaked in ignorance and bravado that renders it necessary to create what is actually nonexistent. I am thinking of an independent self or person residing in the body somewhere, owning the body and calling it 'mine'. It then becomes seduced by its own creation—the narcissist of narcissists, if you like.

In a way, it has not made a mistake, this is what comes with the territory. It is useful to tell a lie and know someone else cannot read your thoughts. The trouble is that self creates the notion of non-self and so a world out there gets created by default. There is no escaping it.

It can feel mighty uncomfortable, though, to be pushed around by people you perceive as 'other' in a huge, ancient pre-existing universe. You feel a temporary part, a visitor on an alien planet. Life becomes serious business.

The searching, though, is life searching, life getting depressed and life getting frustrated. It is a game, a game that is taken very, very seriously. Once seen, this game is breathtaking. The mind could never have come up with this one. Who sees...? Life sees, that is who.

Your experience is the only one you know of. Use it, do not lose it. Non-separation is all that is re-discovered. Wholeness sees itself in its apparent forms and greets itself round every corner. I invite you to be brave and take a look. When you look with honesty you only see yourself.

The world is my mirror. Reflect on that!

Looking at What Is

We believe there is something called 'space'. Not only outer space, but the space around us. Now, in this space there are things — objects. We are convinced these objects have a life of their own: they have independent existence. In this way a sense of permanence is created in order for planning to take place; for future events to occur; for 'life' to happen. This seems so self-evident that any idea to the contrary feels ridiculous. This is the world of the individual, the person, the 'me.' What follows is an attempt to see if this is true. I don't want to put anything else in its place. If we cannot confirm this commonsense axiom through enquiry, what shall we do? If the very ground of conventional existence can be questioned and shown to be unsound, then like a bouncy castle with the valve open, it starts to deflate and change shape. If you see reality as it actually is, you are in for a shock. You will get over it and a sense of normality will return, but you will never go back to ignorance. The reason is because there is no one to go back and no back to go to.

The world as it appears is the only world you will ever know. Trying to escape this world for some special one made from just awareness or consciousness is not possible. The illusion is all we have. There is no such thing as awareness or consciousness without an object. Have you ever experienced an apple and at the same time been absent? It does not make sense, does it?

And yet awareness gets bandied around in some spiritual circles as if it is the ultimate goal or the absolute. Thinking of awareness or consciousness in this way is the catalyst and impetus for a lot of seeking activity. Awareness seeking seems so much better than everyday life. Everyday life is problematic, messy and untidy, even when we think we have imposed some sort of order or control. We want something with smoother edges and more symmetry. This is not to say that 'something' is not always present even in deep sleep and prior to birth. It is just that deep sleep and prior to birth have a habit of looking after themselves. What we are interested in is this appearance business, this world that keeps showing up that intrigues and scares us in equal measure. Consciousness has the ability to disguise itself and ignore itself when it appears as a world. It is truly astounding the lengths it goes to in order to appear lost in its own creative abilities.

Trying to escape from this conventional world you have come to know will only add to the anxiety and frustration when you are attempting to realise something else called awareness or the absolute. I guarantee you that even after the most illuminating satsang or mind-blowing retreat, you will still need to eat, sleep and use the bathroom. The sun will still burn you and the wind will dry your skin. That is how it is. That is how things are.

Perhaps you can then just relax into the mystery of things and surrender to the All Powerful. But there is no mystery to life; there is just life. To know where it came from, and why, is not possible, simply because that needs 'two' and there is only 'not two'. If you knew what the world is and where it came from, that would only be more fantasy created by a mind that thrives on stories. If you knew the 'secret', then you would think you were godlike, and that would make you very poor company. Thinking you know what anything actually is, is what got you into this mess in the first place.

There is nothing wrong with seeking. The problem is finding, or even not finding, and making a big thing of that. Finding what you are looking for is the worst thing that can happen. The reason is simple: it is bogus!

If you are one of these people who discover the truth as a result of your intense investigations, the chances are you will try and pass it on to others — you know, to save them the trouble of going through what you have been through. This is how the spiritual market place gets erected. Practices and rituals become a 'path' to enlightenment.

But even the messages that say there is nothing to find, that you are it, have the potential to set the mind off again by contemplating nothingness. Now to sit and meditate on nothingness is madness. You are being very unkind to the mind. It will try and help and then start coming up with gobbledygook to support you and your endeavours. You will then get angry with the mind and wish it would just go away — very unfair to something that is just being true to its own nature.

There is only one erroneous, insidious and down-right terrifying idea: that is believing and feeling oneself to be a separately existing thing.

If you are one of these truth seekers it is because, for some unfathomable reason, that feeling of separateness has played the leading role in the drama you call your life. Not everyone experiences separation the way you do. Some get on with their lives sometimes feeling happy, sometimes less so. And even if all their worldly pursuits are a form of seeking, it does not grip these people to the extent that they continually contemplate existence and being. They simply get on with their lives. There is no need for retreats and ashrams for these guys. They are not in a state of bliss, but they are not obsessed with themselves either.

Your obsession with you is the problem. Of course I am talking about the objects of your dream, not 'real' people with 'real' lives. I am talking about the belief in the solidity and permanence of the dream that feels out there and separate. It is not. It cannot be. This is what separation amounts to — a sense of otherness.

You can do nothing more than accept things as they are. How could you do otherwise? Seeking is seeking for something that is 'other', something separate, and, like Father Christmas, there isn't one.

If you want anything to do, do this: the next time you see, touch, smell, taste or hear an apple, ask yourself if any of those experiences can happen in your absence. If not, where is the 'apple'? The answer to this question is highly personal and might not be available in words. It is like watching a child playing with his trucks in the sand-pit and asking his thoughts on awareness or conscious-ness. He'll look at you, smile and then absorb himself once more in building a sand dune or refilling his lorry at his depot. What you cannot see is that he is given you the best answer you will ever get. The difficulty is, you are looking for more.

Liberation is like having one of those fairground grabbers come along, pick you up, take you somewhere neutral, spring clean you, coat you with an anti-static spray and then throw you right back into the thick of it. Only this time, although everything appears just like before — nothing seems to really stick.

The world is appearance only: it has no reality or power of its own. Without no-thing, some-thing cannot appear. Without appearance there is no no-thing to even be contemplated. This is why there is only Wholeness. However, I shouldn't bother contemplating Wholeness — you will only turn it into something objective. When you do that there will appear to be a division into two. Just thought I would save you the trouble, that is all.

Trying to describe this to someone locked into the consensus reality that most people share is not possible. There is a blindness that will not allow any consideration of reality being other than what they have been brought up to believe. To be a person is to see a world that is fully formed and extended in time and space. Objects seem to have inherent existence, an existence that seems to require no cognition. Amazing! What a trick! A moment's reflection, however, brings this assertion into question and renders it impossible. This impossibility arises not because it is too far-fetched, but because the very appearance of anything is the appearance of knowing, experiencing and presence.

Relatively Speaking

Relatively speaking there is a 'me' and a 'you' and it would be silly to say there is no distinction. However, if we look closely, a so-called other person from your perspective — which is the only one you have — can only appear in your consciousness.

They appear in the form of vision, in the form of sound, smell, touch, and if you are really intimate with someone, taste as well. But these all constitute experience. And experience is just another way of saying right now, presently, actually. So, you see, the world of separate things having an independent existence is why some traditions call the world an illusion. They are not saying the world is not appearing; it is just there is no world that can be grasped and described without referring to sensations. This is why you may hear some say that all there is is Wholeness. This is what is being pointed at — one seamless reality that appears as experience in and as awareness. There is not awareness *of*; there is just awareness *in* all its many appearances. Awareness comes with appearances: no appearance, no awareness; no awareness, no appearance. Neither can be grasped without the other. Both are empty. No need to contemplate which has more reality. Not two. Non-dual. Oneness.

The mind could therefore be seen as a kind of projector, peddling fantasy as solid and real, out there and separate. It assigns experience as objective and independent. There is nothing actually wrong with fantasy. Telling our children that Santa delivers presents in the world on Christmas Eve is fun and creates a sense of joy and wonderment. Still believing in Santa as an adult when all the evidence indicates otherwise is downright foolish. But this is what we do when we believe objects have inherent existence—when we believe that they exist in and of themselves without being perceived by us.

It is this very belief that wreaks so much havoc, suffering and anxiety in our lives. But calling the idea of separation just a belief does not capture the accompanying feelings and lived experience of being alone in a vast universe, a universe we have to continually bargain with to give us satisfaction and keep at bay the dark underlying fear that we can be destroyed, and be no more—annihilated.

Ask yourself if you can experience prior to sensation. It would be like saying I knew myself before the body appeared, before my parents got their thing together and initiated that chain reaction that I call myself. It does not make sense. And yet thoughts of an afterlife and going somewhere can grip us with the kind of fear that leads to depression, anxiety, worthlessness—madness. There is nowhere to go other than right here, and 'here' is not a place; it is everything.

There seems to be an implicit idea or assumption that we come into this world as if there is some kind of holding area that keeps us back until we get assigned our era and social background. But if we take the time to investigate, the body has always been right here, at least in potential, inseparable from planetary activity. No new atoms have appeared labelled 'me'. Whatever constitutes the body is assembled from what already is. We do not come into this world; we emerge out of it. This is quite, quite different. We therefore have no separateness or solidity. We cannot find what we are other than an expression of all there is. A unique expression of Wholeness is not a separate being. That is the illusion. That is the error. That is the suffering.

So there is no need to search for your true nature because you do not have one. 'True nature' is just the mind off on another wild goose chase, always trying to make something out of nothing, always trying to have a vantage point and acquire knowledge of this No-thingness. See the futility of this. Laugh at it, then go and hug someone or have a beer.

The advice here is investigate, investigate, investigate. Do not accept anything you hear or read. It will not work. Reality is staring you in the face, and what is staring you in the face is where you begin and end. Take a look. Be brave. Turning inwards and finding emptiness is indescribable — thank goodness. For there is no need to describe something you already are. This is being, Wholeness, oneness. It is beyond description, not because it is too amazing, but because no description can capture it. Capturing This wouldn't be It. It would be just more ideas, beliefs, concepts. It would be soaked in memory, in deadness, in the past. Reality is now; now is reality, again — not two, non-dual, Wholeness.

Warning: take no notice of any message that says,'Who can do that?' Or, 'Who will investigate?' Even though it seems paradoxical, do not let the absence of a 'you' stop you from ripping out the root of suffering. In this play, an apparent character can look at himself, or herself, and question the author's authenticity because they are one and the same. The playwright, the play, and all the characters are not separate. Wholeness searches, Wholeness plays. There is no other.

Relax, you don't have to do anything; you are being done. But have your life. Continue to respond by name, continue to argue with your spouse and get exasperated at your kids. Take a walk in the park and marvel at a tree, a squirrel, a litter bin and a drunk. Feel sad at the plight of the homeless and starving. Hold nothing back. Let actions proceed and watch the hand reach into the pocket and throw a few coins down into the threadbare old hat, by the blanket, by the dog, by the doorway. No need to say it is all an appearance. It is life.

It is a curious thing: when the world shows up, I show up. Or the other way round: when I show up, so does the world. That has always been the case, but largely ignored, unnoticed. This intimate relationship is what has been described as 'nothing appearing as everything', Neither 'everything' nor 'nothing' is deemed to be more important or special — they are one and the same. This is how things actually are. Objects do not turn up without you, how could they? The very first sensation experienced as a baby — and there's a 'you'. Experience is appearing as hunger, as agitation, as wanting to be held. By not expecting things to be a certain way or searching for a special state, you become bullet proof, because whatever turns up is nothing other than experiencing appearing as 'that'.

At first it is destabilising. You are questioning objective existence and doubting assumptions about reality; you are questioning assumptions which have been spoon-fed to you all your life. This destabilising is unavoidable. Some people experience more, some experience less of this destabilisation, but it will be felt; it comes with the territory. For years you have probably accepted that people, places and general everyday objects exist in the way you assumed they did. This is the dream you awaken from, but it is also the one you awaken to. Nothing changes, the sun still rises and the clouds still empty their watery cargo when you have planned your barbecue. The difference is you know you are not separate from the rising sun or the sausages smoking away on the half lit charcoal.

Events and their contents are like a mirror. The images in that mirror, although highly varied, have a strange, unchanging character — they only reflect Wholeness, a kind of full emptiness.

It is one thing to read or be told how human life begins: one solitary sperm fusing with one solitary ovum and starting a series of actions and reactions that never stop even when the body changes function at death. It is quite another to actually witness a baby making an appearance. What you see is the full force and awesome power of nature in one relatively tiny, helpless organism we have dubbed 'baby'. There, staring you in the face, is the miraculous. Yet it so quickly gets taken for granted once all the activities are set in motion to ensure the survival of 'baby' in a world that can produce the miraculous and also destroy it at whim.

Babies are just one example. Take a look at anything and ask yourself, 'If I remove the label from this object and do not replace it, what do I find? What can I say about it?' Try this and if you can let go or see beyond preconceptions, you might see that objects are not objects; they are the appearance of no-thing, appearing as whatever is appearing. Gone is the idea of the inherent existence of objects, and in its place a mystery unfolds. A mystery that has always been here, dancing in front of us, showing us its wares as well as fooling around with notions of permanence and solidity.

Nothing can be taken away from its environment and still continue intact and unchanged. Stick a human being in outer space without any artificial environment, such as a space suit, and you will quickly find that the normal functioning has been arrested to the point of failure. Oxygen which abounds on earth is absent in outer space. The body, interacting with these conditions, will very quickly be no more.

So in describing any particular aspect of the world you are also describing the universe as it exists today. We have become so narrowly focused on objects as things in themselves and defined by words, that to consider interconnectedness and Wholeness seems fanciful and a pursuit for those with their head in the clouds; sane, responsible people knuckle down and get on with things.

It is just this sanity, this 'normality', that becomes problematic and stifling. It is the constant feeling of being just a cog in a machine playing our little role that starts to fatigue us to the point of desperation or depression and anxiety.

Then, the very system that confuses us also supplies the means to fix us and help us play the game differently, by offering the wisdom of professionals well versed in the trials and tribulations of life in the form of therapeutic intervention. This system is born out of ignorance but it attempts to help the poor soul afflicted by doubt and fear to see the world differently, more accurately, with more clarity.

What is not seen by the client/patient is that the veil is still tightly attached; it has just been decorated with nicer designs and a few more holes inserted to enhance breathing and ensure a better exchange with the conditions of the preformatted world of reality. It seldom occurs to either the helper or the helped that the world we know and love is constructed rather than interacted with. And so the game goes on, perhaps a little easier and with more accuracy, but the root cause remains to emerge again in another guise with new obstacles to overcome in the future. Even those therapies that operate within the paradigm of phenomenology cannot shake off an independently existing world with a unique interpretation by its interlocutor, negotiating using a pseudo-exchange of ideas to arrive at closure.

Rules of Grammar Are Not Necessarily Rules of Nature

Just because our English teacher taught that nouns refer to objects that are responsible for the doer of actions does not mean we can actually find correlates in the environment that support this socially constructed belief born from modern day grammar. Simply put: a snooker ball exists as a pattern of light, touch, sound, smell and taste. It emerges from current conditions. Conventionally we can say the rolling and point of contact caused the object ball to change location, but this simply describes activity, a happening, rather than one object striking another. We therefore confuse current activity with independently existing entities.

An Atheist Looks to a Christian for a Sense of Identity and Vice Versa

Friends create enemies and enemies create friends. You can never know only one pole of anything. In fact to know is to be aware of this dualism, but neither of them exists independently. Waves consist of crests and troughs; mountains need their valleys. To omit either is to destroy them both. So duality is a celebration of Wholeness and not something to be avoided or dismissed by an appeal to nihilism. This is what a person can never see, even though it continually stares him or her in the face and taps them on the shoulder at every opportunity. To be a person is to be contracted, a real sense of me in here and you out there — but not just a 'you' out there. Every single thing from a sandwich to a sand-fly seems to have its own independent reality, totally divorced from 'me as a person' and my private existence that must be kept under wraps at all costs.

This mental trickery the brain performs seems to be the only game in town, and coupled with everyone playing the same game, it is no wonder we feel lost and adrift on a wide and vast ocean not of our making. To be a person is to strive to fit in and be accepted by the community that feeds and educates and expects returns in equal measure or, more often than not, in even greater measure.

The depression, hopelessness and constant underlying anxiety that plague us day in day out have the power to be our saving grace. This unease, the feeling that something's just not right here, can be the return home to a place we never left; the yellow brick road stops its winding course to reveal a hint of its circularity.

Separation never feels ok — ever. Do not listen to anyone who says separation's fine because all there is is Wholeness. It will not wash! Separation is a longing to return, to come home, to re-establish the embrace that enveloped us from our ignorant beginning. This is never a discovery in a novel sense as, say, when a scientist discovers a new particle. No, this is a re-discovery. That is why this is already absolutely known and not the mystery we thought it was.

To come home is to notice what is here now, not what can be achieved through effort and practice. This is to look with the eyes of a child and the wisdom of an adult. Nothing new is presented to us, we just simply see nakedly without trying to get something, achieve something, and distort something. Watching the bee collect her nectar from the seducing, enticing flowerhead, leaves you dumbstruck, and the recognition that this activity has its counterpart in the cooperation of your heart with your brain shows you Wholeness without words, without satsang — without gurus. This is nature's gift to itself. It is seeing itself and it is being itself. Nature laughs at itself with a guffaw that can shake the pillars of heaven. See yourself in the cry of a new-born, in the heat of the sun and the taste of a beer on a hot day on the patio. Nothing appears without you, and you cannot be seen unless you wear a disguise. No need to give special treatment to still-ness, it is over here, in the movement of life!

Mind

I want to look at something which I hope you do not think so obvious as to require no explanation. I want to explore what we mean by 'mind'. Ordinarily the word is used to describe some kind of private activity like working a maths problem out in our head or wondering where to go on the next holiday. We can have 'a lot on our mind' or even feel we are 'losing our mind.' So, I guess we could reserve the definition for some private activity that only the thinker has access to.

I want to extend this definition, though, simply because I do not think it is comprehensive enough. Look at an object, any object, and see what it is made of. I am going to take the tape measure lying on my desk as my example. I notice its shape as curved at one end and straight at the other. It is black in colour with splashes of yellow. It feels a reasonable weight, maybe getting on for 500 grammes. It smells a bit plastic-like and I'll leave the taste for now: it is been in my pocket and everywhere! Extend the ruler and it sounds metal-like and a bit squeaky. The point is I have not described it without appealing to all the senses I have at my disposal. I have used thinking to gain some sort of description for you. Every one of these seem separate, don't they, but separate from what? If these senses

17

fell away, I would find it mighty hard to hang on to the object I call tape measure. What I am getting at is that mind activity also includes the appearance of objects in the world. The remarkable thing is that we assign an independent existence to these objects. In other words, we believe they exist when the senses aren't at work. So, if I am concentrating on cooking the dinner, I assume the tape measure is sitting on the desk in the form I previously described. This is not my experience and never has been. The tape measure is empty of its own existence. It appears when I say it does and at no other time.

I know this does not sound overly exciting and not quite Rumi's ecstatic poetry or Tao Te Ching stuff. Nevertheless, there can be no objects in reality. Objects exist in fantasy only. But fantasy is no other than reality appearing as fantasy. There is no such thing as unreality. If you have started to release smoke out of your ears, then take a breather. I am not suggesting anything new is occurring, all I am saying is that reality is not what we have assumed it is. The reality for the individual who thinks he lives on a planet in the universe is a story; it is a dream. This is what a person cannot let go of. Because if the consensus view of life goes, so does the person. You cannot get rid of this old notion and remain intact. It is like getting rid of black and keeping white. This is why a seeker can never find what he or she is looking for. It sounds a bit bleak, I suppose, and a bit hopeless as well. But never mind, let us have a go.

The mind is subject to some bad press in spiritual circles, rendering it an inadequate device for self-realisation. We hear things like, 'The mind has not a clue,' or, 'You need to transcend the mind to reach nirvana.' However, the mind, or thinking, is not going away. We need it to function responsibly and intelligently in this world. We need to know our enemies as well as our friends through the amazing cognitive capabilities that match current patterns with older established ones. It is useful to dodge a person in the supermarket who's bored you to tears on a previous encounter and so enable your half hour lunch break to be as productive as possible. The mind is a marvel of nature. The emergence of thought is the emergence of 'world'. Thinking creates novel situations and constant change that appear and disappear almost instantaneously. If we accept the evolutionist theory of life, then we can see physiological change and novelty are considered a gradual tinkering brought about by slow environmental pressures; thinking is not bound by the same time constraints.

The trick is to give it something to do. This way it will be like a sheepdog at your feet waiting for you to throw that tennis ball for the hundredth time. It hates standing still. It gets bored, restless and silly. Give it some homework and mark its results. Be strict, though, it can be very economical with the truth and it is a master of deception. You thought Derren Brown was good? Wait till you see what your own mind is capable of.

Probably the strongest, most ubiquitous belief the mind has is that you, whatever that is, is located inside the body as a person — whatever that is. This, the mind argues, is your ultimate residence, the location from which you view the world and plan your activities for the rest of your life. In here we can hold our secrets and fantasies. We can contemplate whom we would like misfortune to visit and imagine the triumph after defeating our enemies from the past and present in a mock battle that would leave the writers of Star Wars in a daze. Yes, in here no one can see our vulnerabilities; no one can really know we're worthless and unlovable.

But take a look; see where this world where you gain all the ideas for your scripts comes from. Let us start with a big one — other people. Generally other people appear to us as objects. They seem to have clearly defined boundaries and stand out from whichever background is appearing at the time. They match with a previously held pattern that rings the 'human being' or 'person' bell. We then perhaps smile, recoil or greet our object. We make a connection.

Now, give your mind this one to chew on: have you ever witnessed a so-called other person and also been absent? I cannot stress enough that you should answer only from your direct experience. Do not allow thought to create an idea of another person existing in time and space that you are not privy to. The mind cannot help but come up with a very intellectual answer that will take you from here to Timbuktu and back again. It is only trying to help. It wants to find an answer that meshes with some higher order or core beliefs set down at a much earlier time. Do not accept its first answer, give it something else to do. Ask it if anything else is apparent when the other person appears. It might start to have an inkling where this investigation is going. A bead of sweat may appear on its wrinkled, perplexed brow. Keep going. Ask it if there is a sense of knowing or presence indicated in its answer. Just wait for a reply. Be patient. It might play the 'shadow card'.

The shadow card works like this: objects as we know them might not be what we actually see, but there is still something forming an impression on our nervous system. There is still someone inside constructing something outside and creating a mind object, even if that mind object is not a faithful one-to-one match with the thing that is really there. This, to be honest, is not too bad an answer; the mind has done well. If you are a sensitive type, you might feel wounded and deflated at this piece of logical mortar shell aimed in your direction, but congratulate the mind, and just like Columbo as he is walking out the door of a suspect's house say, 'Oh, and just one more thing before I go... '

The mind's answer still requires a kind of knowing, regardless of whether the object is perceived as real or represented. It makes no difference to experience whether it's real, constructed or dreamt; there is still experiencing. Now, experiencing requires something experienced—an event, an object or a memory. Something needs to splash its colour on the canvas; but once splashed on the canvas, try and remove it, allow it to stand on its own two feet. Give the splash of colour its own show, make it the star and be in awe and utter reverence at the sight before you. Then pull yourself together and take off your Bullshitzio Italian designer glasses. You cannot separate the splash of colour, or experience, from experiencing or knowing. They are one and the same. The splash of colour is the canvas colouring. The canvas and the colour are not two things.

You might find a silence from the mind at this stage. Is it re-arming itself or fatally wounded? My answer would be neither: it's in shock, it has probably seen a ghost for the first time and just realised it can put its hand right through it. In other words, an absence has been sensed. The world has started to lose its solidity, its permanence, its created status. Just stop now. Listen to the silence. There is nothing left to do. Any counter attacks now are nothing more than the impact of a child's spud gun —it stings a bit but no long-lasting damage.

The mind has always thought it was running the show called 'me.' It created this person very early on as a way of making sense of the world, a world presented to us from seasoned others in the form of parents and teachers. We not only swallowed our food dutifully, we swallowed their version of reality in the same unquestioning manner. We had no choice. It was a clear case of conform or be ostracised—abandoned.

Survival's quite important for any being, but humans have an astounding level of awareness and sensitivity to their environment, and can respond to challenges with drastic measures and quick reactions. This seems to be the origin of personhood. Rather than feeling ourselves to be everything, we are convinced we are someone; when this happens, the world of others and objects is born. We are now walking through treacle trying to make the best of things but always being slowed down by social goo. Bang goes spontaneity; in come meaning, purpose and duty. Now, rather than *being* life, you *have* a life, and you have to make it work. You must fit in, so as not to be deemed mad or sad. Living becomes a damn serious matter requiring constant maintenance and attention. You are caught in the net of conformity and order. You are expected to play by the rules. You can elaborate a bit and bend them now and again, but you must never look behind the curtain to see the magic man.

This sounds as if there is something deliberate going on, a kind of conspiracy to stop you seeing the truth. It is not. You can walk away anytime you like; the door's open. You just need to be brave and take a look. Most people do not; they are too busy with making their everyday life work

There seem to be pockets of resistance to the reality in which we are conditioned to believe. They are mostly evidenced by a feeling of alienation from the world or a deep curiosity about everything — both of which seem to be conducive to a search for enlightenment. There are people who just cannot make their lives work and there are others obsessed with discovering how the world works. Whatever the reason for the search, it is always a search 'out there', in the world, at the feet of a guru or in the words of a sacred text .

There is a belief that effort brings results for the person, for the individual, for me. So looking seems reasonable and logical. We use methods that we think are tried and tested to reach our goal. What is not seen is that what we are looking for *is* what is looking. The belief that we are imperfect beings who need purification is so strong that we will not hear any message which says we are already all there is. It seems too simple. There has to be more to it than that. It looks much more satisfying, more fruitful, to meditate and chant, to live a pure life and follow the paths trodden by others who will show us the way. Just recognising timeless ever-present is-ness and vibrant energy sounds far too easy.

But life has always been showing us what there is by appearing as a world. It is impossible to see ourselves when there is personal identification and certainty in the way. The thought that we know what we are and what the world is has the power to box us into a corner; it gives us knowledge as a weapon to comfort ourselves and beat the living daylights out of those who will not readily except our version of reality. The quest to get others to see the world the way we do would be a suitable definition for 'power' here, above and beyond the idea of forcing another's body to act in one way rather than another.

When certainty gives way to not knowing, something feels different. It is not easy to put into words, but there is no longer a sense of an independently existing outside world, or even a feeling of just being awareness. The recognition that the appearance of anything is none other than emptiness appearing as form, or nothing being everything, is the straw that breaks the camel's back.

There is no need to chase a particular experience, even if you are trying to regain the blissful time in that last retreat where you dissolved into the cushion and felt all light and airy. No, there is no need.

This is in walking, talking, eating and singing. In fact, whatever shows up, there you are. You are the space that holds, the space that shapes and the space that remains when all the furniture's gone to the second-hand shop.

There is nothing to destroy and nothing to save. The dream carries on with its trials and tribulations. Get involved if you like and play your game. Anxiety may come and anxiety may go. Of course anxiety is not *your* anxiety; it never was. In the same way the person you once identified with as solid and real is seen as just life 'personing', life pretending to be something rather than everything. There is nothing wrong with games; they can be very exciting, something to get the blood rushing and the heart pumping. But there is no need to play all the time. Have a day off now and again and be yourself.

Deep sleep's a great thing: knowing, knowing itself knowingly without object or event. Not a bad way to be. It's even better when you know you are this Now anyway and always have been. Deep sleep does not come and go. It is just got the habit of shaping itself into dreams and other things. It is clever really, changing and staying the same simultaneously. Not one for the logicians among us, granted. But there is such a real obviousness to this that defies all attempts to grasp it and understand it. The thing is you have tried to understand all your life and all it's got you is reading this book, and probably others, hoping for a way out. There is no way out of an imaginary prison or an imaginary maze, though. If this was graspable it would fall through your fingers like soft, dry sand. Grasping is letting go.

Life Anew

There may come a time when all the reading, internet frenzy and meetings in clarity cease to grab your attention. Their draw seems to be waning. The interest has gone and you do not know why. It seems to disappear in the same manner it came, that is, without permission. Rather than reading and re-reading someone else's words, everyday activities and objects become more vivid and sounds become deafening by their presence. Sitting down in the lounge with someone putting away pots and pans in the kitchen feels like they are being knocked on the inside of your head. The sound of an aeroplane's engine, once thought to be far away and distant, shows up in the same place where the pressure of the body is making contact with a seat or nestled against the hunger twinges in the tummy around lunchtime. Nothing is being filtered out by thinking and knowledge. There seems a first time for everything and there is a feeling this has never showed up this particular way before — which, you will discover, it has not. It is as if we had stopped looking and ignored the sheer amazement of being. There is an unfathomability of what there is, right here and not somewhere else over there.

Other people seem closer and you find yourself just allowing them to be themselves and let them behave any way they please. Gone are the old templates you tried to fit on top of them to predict, know and control. You see them more without prejudice and without the usual bias that comes with incorporating the unknown into the apparent known.

There is a kind of relaxation in another's company that you could only have dreamt about before. The envy of competent social performers has given way to a way of being which empowers both you and the chap in your field of vision. In a way this is not surprising because the 'other' is just as much you as the eyes that see him. It is like dolls within dolls within dolls, never ending, reaching into infinity.

More surprising is that the need to talk about the change you have experienced does not arise. There is a keen interest in the everyday that has been absent for so long. Conversations about the state of the economy or the price of carrots seem to carry equal weight and so you can play any game with anyone and not falter from the clarity that comes with liberation. Anything is allowed to show up, nothing is unwelcome. This does not mean there is a rigid response to events close to home like just watching and walking by when someone falls over. Responses happen and the hand reaches out. Concern for other's welfare can actually increases because the bashed knee of the victim leaves a funny kind of graze on your own.

The urge to communicate this realisation can also recede. At one time you may have felt like going up to someone on the street, grabbing them by both shoulders and screaming at them to wake up and see what you see.

There is no need now. There has only ever been you in a sense, and so let the characters in your dream play their parts. Leave them alone. They are fine just the way they are.

There is a Zen saying translated by D.T. Suzuki in his *Essays in Zen Buddhism*: 'Before I had studied Chan (Zen) for thirty years, I saw mountains as mountains, and rivers as rivers. When I arrived at a more intimate knowledge, I came to the point where I saw that mountains are not mountains, and rivers are not rivers. But now that I have got its very substance I am at rest. For it's just that I see mountains once again as mountains, and rivers once again as rivers.'

A puzzling statement for sure, but it has such potency when you have spent so much time trying to reach a state of union by withdrawing from the world to reach a preferred state where you can become special and leave this nasty world full of stress and pesky people. It points to the realisation that there is nothing wrong with the world just the way it is, the way that it appears and has always appeared. There is no attempt to alter anything any more in order to feel better and more secure.

Climb a mountain, sit on a mountain, photograph a mountain, it's all the wondrous play that is showing up and entertaining the audience. Climbing it is not conquering it; it is shaking hands with an old friend that has gone a bit rough round the edges. It is this engagement with the world that you could never have imagined. You were looking for something other than what is. What is, in your naïve opinion, was the cause of all your troubles. How can the very same world afford you so much pleasure now? The secret is that you got out of the way and stopped pushing it around. The twisted knot that got tighter the more you tried to wriggle free has fallen away on its own, releasing the captive to vanish from a place it had never frequented. That is freedom; that is liberation.

It is the simplicity that strikes at the heart of this. Working things out and wanting to control complicates matters. But if you have one of those minds that have to know, you are in for a hell of a time. This is speaking from direct experience. This kind of mind will not tame easily. It is like trying to wrestle a snake into a bottle. A mind like this has to have its nose rubbed into the dirt time and time again. It is like someone grabbing you by the hair and thrusting your head under water, allowing a short breath for confession, refusing, and then thrusting you back in for another round. It is not pleasant and it is not something you would want advance warning of, but that is how it is for some. This enlightenment is not what is on the advertisement flier that you imagined. No cosmic consciousness and blissful fulfillment here!

Perhaps you cannot have someone else's path. Maybe you need to walk in the light rather than in the shadow of someone else. It is very appealing to take a short-cut and download a smart guy's essay. You might even fool your teacher for a while; but you will never kid yourself. That guy can see right through you. He is too close, you see, and never misses a trick.

Favouring the Teacher
Over the Message

It's quite exciting to hear an 'enlightened being' speaking about things that you thought were private and only rattling around in your own head. Having someone grab your attention in this way seems a way out of your prison of misery and despair. Now there is someone you can look up to, someone who really understands, someone who can point the way. It is easy to be seduced into that world, copy the patter and copy their message. You can find yourself hanging on their every word, quoting their sayings to blast other teachings and opinions on forums and blogs. It can be so subtle at times.

The teacher/follower relationship can be almost hypnotic. The mind starts elevating teachers to such high positions that if the non-dual teacher turned to Catholicism half-way through a satsang, some people would follow and look for the hidden meaning. The teacher knows best because they've been where you have not and seen what you have not. Listening to something you have not heard before can be quite powerful at times and keep you coming back for an update or the promise of another layer. But teachers appear in dreams, and if you find yourself sitting at the feet of an enlightened one then not to worry — you have just got one of those kinds of dreams rather than one of the other ones. Liberation follows few rules, I have noticed.

Time

I do not think I could write a book like this one without talking about time.

Time is so wrapped up with thought, it is impossible to talk about time without referring to thinking. As I write this, I am sitting in my van at a retail park watching cars come and go and people either darting in and out of the terrace of shops or sitting at a pavement table sipping expensive coffee. A bloke's just walked by drinking something out of a plastic cup. There are lots of different activities, then, wherever I look.

But what is going on if I am open to what is? Every image is constantly being updated, change is constant, nothing stands still. And how do I know this change? Well, guess what, something here moves not one nanometre — ever. It is this unchanging presence that has always been here, dressing itself up as novelty and change. It is not that something's appearing in my awareness — no. Awareness, or, knowing, is appearing as constant change, constant novelty and constant potential.

This is non-separation. How obvious it is when it is seen. Past and future belong to thought and nothing else. So, where does that leave Now? I suggest we can eliminate Now from our enquiries. You would have more success knitting fog than getting your head round Now. Now is a thought because it is made out of past and future and we have already associated those two with thought.

If someone comes up to you and says, 'Sorry son, it is hopeless. You have no future here,' do not take offence. Thank him for his honesty and walk off with a spring in your step. There has only ever been one thing, which you can call 'present-sensations-of-no-duration'. Sounds, sights, smell etc. constantly appearing and disappearing. You cannot grab this and make it into something. It is like trying to bring that Ferrari out of your dream last night and park it outside. It won't happen.

A clock is a machine with a repeating event: tick-tock, tick-tock. Digital timepieces may change numbers at regular intervals with some other numbers changing occasionally and other numbers staying the same for a while. Imagine that you are standing in front of an ana-logue clock watching the second hand make a complete revolution. We can say the hand is moving and time is flowing — but what is really going on? I suggest the answer is 'nothing'. Nothing happening. There is just the current event of hand movement that plods along in a timeless zone.

Time will appear real while you live in thought and fantasy. Here we can imagine next year's holiday; here we can imagine getting old and dying. Just let this sink in for a while. Be amazed at what is going on. I cannot fathom it. No one can. It is just plain miraculous.

All you ever see is timeless, infinite, unborn, un-created stillness and silence — moving and staying still, changing and unchanging. These gobbledygook statements are why the mind cannot go here; it is out of bounds — no entry. This is reality in all its glory. You will not find yourself anywhere because there is only everything and everywhere. Try and stop life, try and start it. You cannot; it just happens.

You, the person, will never see this, never in a million years. They are incompatible you see; a person is time-based and this is not. If a person is time-based, he is fiction, fantasy and dream stuff. He is no different to the one in your dream being terrorised by Daleks or the one teaching Superman how to fly.

Absence

Absence can be a bit of a shock at first because there is nothing to hold onto. But like falling into a bottomless pit, after a while you can relax and forget about the impact — because it is bottomless and there will never be an impact! I suggest life is like falling, mostly holding onto ideas, thinking they are safety rails, sometimes noticing there are no rails and you are doing just fine. Nothing needs to be held onto — there is not anything to hold.

There's no need for this to get you down; there's no need to withdraw from life. No. You could not if you tried, anyway. When consciousness, when life itself, lets go of thinking that it is something rather than everything, it marvels at itself, celebrates itself in all its forms. There is one canvas here coloured in the most intricate of ways. The paint depicts infinite variety with all its wondrous colours. But take a closer look; it is all made of paint — one scene, one canvas built like an Etch A Sketch. Go and give it a shake, start afresh and draw something else.

Absence is actually made out of presence. If you discover you cannot locate yourself and yet do not disappear in a puff of smoke, then there is a mystery going on. Why is there still something felt? Why is the sun still shining and all the rest of life still turning up? It is simply because all these activities are an expression of what you are. If they are an expression of what you are why should they go away? Everything that appears, including thought and itchy elbows, is Wholeness appearing as that. In a dream there might appear to be lots going on including emotions like fear or ecstasy. But there is only one dream and one dreamer. When you wake up there is no time delay while bits of the dream get put away somewhere special; the whole lot goes together.

I expect you have heard it said that words cannot capture this. Not so. They do just as a good a job as anything else. Wanting them to mean anything is the difficulty. Words on a page or words clothed in sound reflect timeless presence. Seen in this way, words take their place in heaven next to my pint of lager and take-away curry.

My Story

I cannot remember a time when I wasn't anxious. There seemed always something to be worried about. It might be the dentist appointment or the fact that I had broken something belonging to my brother and hid it away in a cupboard, and was sure my crime would be rumbled by someone any day now. Life seemed a constant problem. There was always something going on.

I am the youngest of five boys. My dad always said he didn't know where I came from. He was telling the truth of course, except not in the way he meant it to sound. We owned our own house in a small farming village near Daventry, Northamptonshire, England. I remember the farmer leading his cows down the lane next to our house and watching while one or two fancied their chances of escape and jumped our white ranch fence to leave well formed hoofmarks on the lawn.

In the summer when I was about five years old, I would sit in the back of the corn trailer with a few other kids in the village and watch while the combine shot its booty among our bare feet as we pushed the grain towards the chute for bagging. Summers were hot and life was slow.

As I was the youngest, a clear pattern of family life

and rules preceded my appearance. My parents were working class and we survived through strict money management. My Mum hated living in the village. She was away from the town she grew up in and now lived among people who were a constant topic of behind-doors criticism. This must have caused more friction and atmosphere than my developing self could tolerate. I developed a pattern of absorbing other people's frustrations in an attempt to relieve them of their burden. I turned away from my own joy to provide mental comfort for others in a private world made up of mental characters; this led to depression, anxiety and seeking later on.

Memories of this early time in my life come and go, but the memory of one incident is made of triple reinforced concrete surrounded by a lead-lined box. Something had happened one day and my Mum was in a rage I hadn't witnessed before. She said she'd had enough and was leaving. She opened the kitchen door and walked at great pace down the path that led to the road. I can remember running after her so fast that my legs turned to jelly. I, at 4 or 5 years old, took it on board that I could bring her back. I could sort it out for her. I don't know what I said to her but my reward was being told off for crossing the road without looking. My mum returned after a breather and a visit to the local shop and life simply carried on.

That incident and a few others changed the view I had of people; they were not to be trusted. I protected myself by withdrawing so far within myself and feeling so isolated that spontaneity took a back seat and self-management took its place. This became the pattern that dominated. Life became serious. I suspect this is the same for most people, although our significant events are different.

Schooldays were tough. I hated lessons. I was so tense trying to keep myself from falling apart and feeling so shy and anxious all the time, I had nothing left mentally to study with. All my efforts were to keep at bay this worthlessness and hatred I felt inside. Everyone was smarter, better looking and more comfortable with themselves and other people than I was. There was a longing not to be what the voice in the head was telling me, a longing to really fit in, although I never felt I did. I wasn't too bad at bluffing though. I had quite a few friends but hated others joining the friendship that I thought was exclusively mine. I could not cope with someone new I didn't know muscling in. If they were very sociable and made my friends laugh I would automatically take that to mean that I was boring and uninteresting.

You see, I was living totally in my thoughts. The world had become a hostile place full of mental characters created to make my life a misery. I hated being noticed by anyone. I hated drawing attention to myself. I thought I could hide from life and especially other people. It was as if I were on constant guard to protect this pathetic creature that was sucking the life blood out of me. It continually needed to be fed with reassurance, and if that reassurance was not forthcoming, I would take it as confirmation of my intrinsic worthlessness and badness.

Whenever I met other people it always seemed to result in taking the lower rung of the ladder and looking up at them. They were more important, more intelligent and more worthy of success. This is what separation meant to me. I felt isolated and alone in a very nasty place full of objects, places, buildings and people that were weighing me down more and more.

I left school with no qualifications. I could not engage

with education. I was too scared of it. I could not allow myself to ask a silly question or get something wrong and look a loser in front of anyone. It was as if I said to myself, 'If you do not try too hard there is little chance of not being perfect.' Being perfect was the standard I set myself. Other people were perfect, so I thought, and if they knew something I didn't, the assumption was they had been born with this knowledge and were special. I didn't know and could not risk exploring and showing others what I thought I could hide from them — my worthlessness and utter stupidity.

There was always a battle raging within. Sometimes it was a little disturbance of the peace, at other times — carnage. Resting I could never do; I had to be ready for that surprise attack and fend off anyone with a pass key to the inner locker.

I found some interest and respite while reading about psychology. It was mainly self-help books, but a few others, too, that were more honest about the crazy world we live in. I studied with the Open University at age 30 concentrating on psychology, and after 4 years of hard work I finished with an Upper Second. I was working full time and had just started a family, so it was a good result. Summer schools and class activities were hellish; feelings and memories of being useless returned as soon as I smelt the interior of a place of learning. Once again, I didn't want to say that I didn't understand and this left me to struggle on my own behind closed doors. I received some very good marks and comments, but I never believed them fully. I thought the tutor just felt sorry for me or, God forbid, she liked me. 85% or 95% wasn't perfect and the room for improvement section seemed to be written in red with a rainbow of highlighter pens bordering it, making sure I could notice these comments above any-thing else.

When the course finished I wanted to be a clinical psychologist and help people with issues and problems. I thought I could pass on my new-found knowledge and help them. A few voluntary posts and a bit more study and it fizzled out, leaving me feeling a loser once again. I got really down and depressed and sought therapy for myself. It was scary listening to my own voice in the presence of a stranger discussing some things I wouldn't even admit to myself, but it felt good for a while and life was better.

Trying to fix a ghost does not last long though; they have a habit of evading capture. I decided to get fit and see if exercise could lift me. I read that a good workout would release happy chemicals in my brain and make me feel good, so I enrolled at a gym. Even though I felt self-conscious among all the fit, good-looking people, I managed to make a few friends and chat fairly freely.

I had a personal trainer for a while and started to enjoy life at the gym. It turned out this guy had got a few issues himself regarding drink, and last minute cancel-lations became more and more frequent. One day, after arriving to find my trainer absent without leave again, another trainer, Lynn, offered to train me instead. I accepted, and this is where, believe it or not, my spiritual search began.

We got on well and she seemed interested in some of my ideas about psychology and people. There was something about her: I could not put it into words at the time and cannot now. Out of the blue she dropped a book in my lap. One look at the cover and I saw the words 'spiritual' and 'enlightenment'. I wasn't particularly impressed as it wasn't a subject I would normally choose. I didn't want to seem rude so I took it and sat down that very lunchtime, opened it and looked inside. Whilst turning the pages and chomping on my sandwich, something clicked. Here was someone talking about time and presence and suffering. There were words on the page I hadn't come across before. I turned the pages at great pace, eager to hear more. Something was going on. I had read some pretty interesting stuff whilst studying and in the books I normally bought, but this was different. This was activating an unexplored area. A light went on.

I Googled the author and read a bit more. As with all Google searches, it brought up loads of other relevant stuff. I found myself entering the world of the spiritual seeker. I clicked on and found Tony Parsons, Mooji, Adyashanti, Nisargadatta, Ramana Maharshi, ancient Chinese sages and texts from the past. I found interpretations of Jesus' words pointing to Wholeness rather than a guy with a white beard sat on a throne in a cloudy place. I was hooked. I had been stirred up like one of those Christmas snow storms in a paperweight. This was 2008. I was aged 40.

I was trying hard to really get it but any clarity didn't seem to stick. I thought I got it, but I also felt I was fooling myself as well. I can honestly say, there were times I wished I had never started this crazy stuff. Some days were worse than before: holding my head in my hands staring at my computer screen was not a pleasant posture. But this had a life of its own. I could not stop if I wanted to.

One day, on a chilly November afternoon, I was waiting for my wife outside a supermarket. I didn't want to go in. I was in one of those moods when people seem threatening. As I stood in the doorway alcove, I found myself staring and scanning people coming out of the shop with their bags full of food and stuff. It felt like the scanning had a life of its own. Time stood still and it was like I knew what I was seeing, but at the same time I didn't. This felt weird. I looked away in a strange state. Then, coming towards me and indicating to pull in, was the biggest, reddest, loudest bus I would ever see in my life. It felt like it was parking itself in my chest area and activating every sense I had got at full volume. Then it ended and I was in shock. My wife appeared and I said nothing.

I tried to recreate this event over the next few years. It had felt good. *Is that what non-separation is like?* I thought. This I could enjoy. I didn't go to meetings of non-dual or spiritual teachers, I just continued exploring this on the internet and watching YouTube videos. I emailed a few guys whom I thought I resonated with. I did try and speak to people close to me, but they didn't really get it and I simply shut up and kept quiet.

One Saturday, I got up like any other. I had no plans to do anything and so just went on the internet to see if I had missed anything obvious in all those words, methods and teachings. I clicked on Tony Parsons' site and saw he had a meeting planned that day in London. I live about 90 miles away, but found myself driving to the station, catching the train, and two hours later sat in the Hampstead Friends' Meeting House, listening to this man speak about... well, nothing. I had no questions because I kind of had a feeling what the answer might be. I just listened, spoke to no one and left three hours later. I didn't know what was exactly being pointed to. But I was certain about one thing: I would never return to a meeting about this. If I was going to see what all the fuss was about, it was a journey I would take without a travelling buddy.

Then, one day, I just *saw*. I saw that the idea of anything separate — separate people, places and objects out there in a separate world — is untrue. This was absolutely known without any doubt. After that there was just a total absence of time, purpose, and silly stories. The world gave up its secrets. There is no separate person here having a life. There is just life. Life, with its amazing array of expressions, swirling and turning in a timeless zone that has always been the case. All appearances are the One, appearing as many in a dance that never ceases, continually displaying itself, disguising itself, playing with itself. Objects are no longer objects; people are no longer people. Nothing can be pinned down and known. Nothing conforms to the crazy notions that plagued the individual person you thought you once were. Drinking a coffee and feeling the sensation and smelling the aroma are just totally stunning. Watching a duck paddle away on the water is spellbinding stuff. And as the watching's going on, nothing's really happening, nothing's leaving its mark anywhere. All trails are being refreshed with new ones, constantly, unceasingly.

Normal everyday functioning is not affected. Watching television, cooking the dinner, taking the kids to parties and teeth cleaning continue. It is just that, well, that is all that's happening, no more and no less. The drama goes on and everything continues to appear — except that somewhere it is known there are no things out there and separate; they are right here in the place you never left — Wholeness. The character that apparently masquerades as a personal entity gets released from its prison and on release it melts into everything like a drop of rain landing on the surface of the ocean. The character remains full of life, energy and freedom that enables it to say and speak whatever pops into its head with very little filtering and checking beforehand. There is a sense of aliveness that no person could ever imagine. Life is full-on. Life is a scream.

Games

Do you like games? I do. I remember playing Monopoly as a kid with my brother in the summer holidays. Hours we would spend as property tycoons down in the smoke, buying places we would never afford in real life. We used to bend the rules as well, borrowing money off the bank with a zero interest rate and no limit on the advance. I am sure my brother's stash grew a bit when I went to the loo. He said I imagined it.

Games can cause adrenaline to rise and tempers to fray. Whilst we are immersed in them they take on a reality of their own and reactions to our opponents can imitate the feelings one gets by being exposed to stressors out there in the real world, such as someone pinching your parking space after you have been good and waited your turn.

Is this so-called life any different? I would say not. We just never know when to put the board away. The play becomes so real because we give it power. Life becomes a task, something to achieve. Games have one up on the real world: there is usually a clear goal and so we know what we want to achieve and what it will look like when we get there. The trouble with seeking is that we are searching for... we cannot really say what. It is something to do with contentment or happiness, or one-ness with everything. Staying in the now is a good one, and perhaps shutting that noisy mind down for good would be a goal for seeking.

But we do not change the rules of Monopoly so much that it becomes pointless. Yes, we can conjure up one or two variations to speed things up a bit, but we would get bored with it if the challenges disappeared. We do want life to change, though. We want it to look a certain way and for people to behave in a way we feel is somehow more conducive to an egalitarian or utopian idea that we have read about in a book somewhere.

This is swimming against the current. All it will do is make you tired, because no matter how hard you swim upstream you will never reach home. You will end up grappling for the river bank to rest and have another go when you have got your strength back. What we cannot see is that we could stay on the bank in the deck chair and saunter back home when our legs feel like it, or let the current carry us along with it. Either way there does not seem to be much resistance: the legs move us from A to B and the stream will take us along with it for the ride. If we can sit back and enjoy the thrill of the current, we might explore places we would never have the guts to visit ourselves. The same caravan holiday every year might start to appear a bit bland if the stream chooses our destination for us.

I do not wish to overdo the metaphors, but seeing that life just happens regardless of what we think about it brings a strange feeling of relief as the knots of anxiety loosen and drop away.

The Lucid Dream

If you have not had a lucid dream or have had one and didn't know what to call it, I'll try and describe it here. A lucid dream is when there is a kind of knowing that you are dreaming. It is like having your foot in both camps — the waking world and the dream world. I remember a dream where I found myself under a sink fiddling with the plumbing. As I got up from the crouching position to find a wrench, I noticed that I was in a room with freshly plastered walls and no doorway. I looked around for a while thinking: '... what the f*** is going on here.' It then dawned on me I was having a dream. For a while the sense of power is immense. It is like feeling invincible because you know that, whatever happens, not a damn thing is going to affect or hurt you in any way. Unfortunately, it seems you cannot stay in two worlds at the same time for long. After it gets rumbled it simply fades away to waking up, and leaves a residue and sense of wonderment and unease. It is rather puzzling for a while, but soon gets erased by the everyday task of making life work again — kids, work and shopping, that kind of thing.

If we remain open for a while, though, this experience can show us something. The dream world appeared real. There was an experience that was, at least at first, very mundane, worldly; until there is an inconsistency, everything seemed pretty normal. When the appearance, in this case the dream, is seen to be not what it appears to be, it is only a stone's throw away to revealing the same about the so-called real world in which we apparently wake up. Look and see the appearances; they are flashing around in the same way they were in the dream. People are walking by and we can still fiddle with the plumbing under the sink if we want to. But we can see that appearances are showing up as experiencing, just like the dream.

Experiencing is still experiencing whether we can walk out of a kitchen doorway after changing the tap washer or ponder how we found ourselves in a place with four walls and no door. It is the same. Whatever shows up, it is all experiencing. Nobody is experiencing; there is just experiencing, but a belief in personhood prevents this kind of seeing, prevents this 'pure' experiencing. Thinking of ourselves as being someone will only allow for ignorance — nothing else. Ignorance seems to be a world of time and space, of becoming something in the future. But here is the thing: ignorance is no other than Wholeness appearing to be ignorant. There is only Wholeness so what else could it be?

Wholeness seems to love its games and plays with itself endlessly. You could say it is like a grand case of cosmic masturbation! But like playing with yourself, you cannot sustain it forever. You get worn out and need a break. You need to come back to reality and mingle a bit. Reality is noticing that appearances, whatever they are and making no distinction, are made out of knowing or being. It does not have to look a certain way or feel a certain way. Whatever shows up, there you are. Not you,

Joe Bloggs the person living in space and time who will die one day and be gripped with remorse about deeds both done and not done at the point and after death. No, all there is, ever has been and ever will be is timeless, being/Wholeness, appearing as whatever is showing up. The drama appears as worlds, galaxies and everything. It appears as hopes, fears, fun and depression too.

The seeing of timeless presence seems to allow for relaxation and just a total stopping of future time. Life as a task loses its appeal and being with 'what is' satisfies whatever it is that sees. Anxiety is transformed into allowing things to happen without trying to shape or own them in some way. Depression turns into simple joys like watching a bird in flight or a dog jumping into the river for the umpteenth time. But we do not have to just revel in the so-called natural world: cups and saucers and bits of rubbish compete on a level playing field now, nothing is any better than anything else. If you have been to India and stayed in an ashram or hitchhiked your way to the current enlightened guy, you have not wasted your time. It is just that that was appropriate and what happened, happened. Your dream's different from mine, but there is only one dreamer.

Repeat Performances

Spiritual experiences, where the old world transforms into something special and we feel *special,* have a habit of leaving you just when the going gets good. We might have started describing our experience hoping to save someone else the trouble of seeking and get them on our own wavelength instead. There might be a sense of knowing what enlightenment is now. We think we can taste what Ramana Maharshi tasted, walk in his shoes and see the world as golden light only. But Ramana's shoes, like Gandhi's, are just smelly old flip-flops when we stick them on. They do not really fit but we will cope with the pong and the pinching so as to keep up appearances and not let anyone down again.

I remember when I had great times as a child, on holiday or a nice day out: afterwards I would descend into an uncomfortable state of loss, and longed for the clock to run backwards. I felt like I had just had a spell out or prison for good behaviour. It was as if I had to return to keeping my head down now and do my time — until the next time. Unlike a prison term, though, this sentence has no release date, no parole and no pardon. You will never be free from this. You never see the prison guard either, but know he is there because you believe you can hear the jangle of his keys and the sound of his footsteps on that cold concrete corridor just outside your cell. You never notice the absence of the cell door or the constant flow of fresh air. You have convinced yourself of your own bad behaviour that has landed you in this slammer.

Wanting something to return just like before never works. Have you ever been on holiday somewhere and had a fantastic time: the weather was good; the food was perfect and the people you met could not have been more fun? When you get home you cannot stop thinking about it and put your relatives through unknown hell when the photos come out and the anecdotes have a life of their own, describing things one way one day and adding a bit the next. Book and find yourself there the following year and it is not the same. Yes, it seems much the same, but the emotional content will not agree with last year's trip. It is a bit disappointing.

I suggest that looking for something in particular through spiritual endeavour ends up the same. Old experiences need constant maintenance. You have got to be on your guard for squatters in the form of new thoughts, ideas and the latest ramblings from the internet. Keeping these changes at bay is exhausting. You have become hyper-vigilant again. This time, instead of keeping that unpredictable world out you had experienced for years, you are now lumbered with a vision of enlightenment that is looking jaded and a bit murky. What started off as the experience to end all experiences has left you with doubt, depression and further dismay. *Oh, no! Seeking's returned*, you say to yourself. You do not appear as vocal at the meetings anymore and you are reading those esoteric scriptures again. *Bollocks, I thought that had finished.*

What the person cannot see is that novelty and change are the spice of life.

Wanting something to conform to our ideas is like trying to fix templates to them and then becoming frustrated when they do not fit. This is expectation and prediction at work — something the mind does incredibly well. It is this function of the mind that allows the body to protect itself from potential danger and lay down patterns for possible future occurrences. There is nothing wrong with this; it is very wise. Appealing to thought to recreate the emotional content associated with happiness and wellbeing, though, is not the same as protecting the body from danger, such as not crossing the road when a juggernaut's approaching or ducking down when a cricket ball's got your name on it. It is like using an adjustable spanner to open a tin of peas; it will not do it. It is the wrong tool for the job.

An appeal for repetition, then, is hopeless. This is not a problem. It only feels this way because the person wants something to hang onto, something to soothe and calm him or her, like an ancient security blanket that smells of Mummy and lots of cuddly things. Repetition is old news, stale and uninteresting. Now is where all the action is. Present being is more alive than any thrills and spills that require language and nuance to recreate and transmit. This is why leaving a retreat or meetings in togetherness fail to deliver when you get back to work on Monday or see the Missis again. They are too old news, too stale and tasteless. Chuck 'em away like mouldy old bread. If you persist on eating such crap it will only poison you.

The Self

The self is one of those terms we slip into our everyday conversations and use it in many, many ways. We say, 'I have hurt myself.' Or, 'I feel self-conscious.' We can talk of self-loathing or self-knowledge. Whilst studying for my degree, I found that the self was defined in different ways by different scholars working within different paradigms (underlying assumptions about what the world consists of and how it holds together). Their starting points were different and the kind of animal they were describing differed too. Some concentrated on cognition or making sense of the world through interpretation and stored knowledge. Others concentrated on actual lived experience for the individual — a phenomenological approach. The psychodynamic line of enquiry focused upon unconscious processes and early childhood emotional development. Another emphasised the social construction of the self, arguing that it emerges from interaction in the world, through language usage and cultural norms.

You can see it is a term that will not be defined once and for all, and yet it is worth examining more closely, just for the sake of breaking down certainty once more and questioning the very fabric of the world we adopt on our arrival and during our stay on the planet. There are so many definitions and perspectives but, for the purposes of *The World Is My Mirror*, we shall be looking at the psychodynamic approach.

You are probably familiar with Sigmund Freud and his idea that the unconscious, rather than being just a storehouse for old experiences and memories, was dynamic and active, influencing current behaviour and directing our thoughts and providing the emotions. Free will was replaced by dark forces that needed to be controlled by psychic structures. It was the everyday strategies we use to keep this equilibrium that were the origin of all behaviour. He argued that we were largely unaware of this battle within: only the quirky behaviour resulting from it that kept turning up brought it to notice.

Freud was quite rigid with his theory and wasn't keen on others developing his original thesis too far. He was interested in tension reduction and the lengths to which we go in trying to maintain equilibrium or pleasure. However, dissenters there were, and other practitioners working within this paradigm noticed that the mind seems to be full of mental characters that populate the internal world and play out their parts in this private space rather than actual people in the here and now. It was argued that our first relationship patterns set up basic templates or caricatures of other people.

As adults we simply fit people into these templates, not consciously of course, but automatically. For example, if we had a strict, punitive father who criticised us, we spend most of our time as adults looking for approval and comfort. We might see all authority figures from our teachers to our bank manager in the same way and return to a time when we felt vulnerable and scared. The point is the world we think we live in is constructed from thought. We do not see anything as it is actually appearing; we are always living in a drama with characters that bear only a slight resemblance to their actual identity. Of course, the people you come into contact with are also doing this, so we end up living out the drama rather than actual lived experience. It seems dramas are interacting with other dramas and distorting everything and everyone. What a mess!

This is referred to as 'living in a closed loop' with repeating patterns, like a mouse on an exercise wheel. This could account for the feelings I had around other people. I never actually saw them; I was slotting them into character, dressing them up in fantasy and mayhem and running the story that was familiar to me rather than simply being and enjoying contact.

This, for me, is why the world appeared stunning on that November day outside the supermarket. I hadn't really seen people and objects before; I was running on old pseudo-knowledge; fitting people and objects into what I thought I knew about the world. This Richard Bates manifestation thought he knew what the world was: he didn't.

When the personal entity is rumbled and Wholeness sees, the world is always refreshing itself in timelessness. Nothing appears the same, ever. Only a cock and bull story created by old templates and memories creates the illusion of permanence and stability. When you walk your dog past your neighbour's house and you stop to speak to him, you have never seen each other in this way before. Not one handshake or smile is repeated. There is just the present configuration of Wholeness or no-thingness. This is a completely different way of being. This is freeing.

I suspect our early years were like this until life got serious. However, as I have said already, to look with eyes of a child and the wisdom of an adult is breath-taking.

The Old and the New

We count the days, months and years and mark off our calendars. History programmes show us ancient lands and monuments and describe a time quite different from our own. We are exposed to older cultures and shown the progressive stages man has superseded to reach his current incarnation.

If you found yourself in Egypt you might be marveling at the pyramids of Giza. Your tour guide is rambling on about who built them and how old they are. You look at your watch to see how much longer to lunch time; you have not eaten since 7 a.m. and you are gagging for an Egyptian beer. You look at your watch, the wrist it is sitting on and the fat bloke on the camel who raises an inward smile. The mind is convincing us that there are separate objects appearing all with varying ages and histories. The separate person is convinced that there was a past when all this was built, a time before this one. It is not true; it is a story appearing at the same time everything else is. The hunger, the thirst, the voice of the guide, the wristwatch complete with wrist and the magnificent structures are all the present appearance of everything. Nothing is any older than anything else. They all appear as this one whole dream about people, places, structures and other times. You can wake up whenever you like or snooze a few more decades and get engrossed in the story. Noticing this is stunning. There are no pyramids four thousand years old. Just like that vintage sports car you won in last night's dream game, it is all just dreaming consciousness, spinning its yarns, having fun with itself.

It is so hypnotic, this life we think we have, so mesmerising. I do not blame anyone scoffing at this and branding me unbalanced. This sounds crazy to the mind; it will not go here. Have you ever been to the vets and seen an owner dragging their dog into the surgery once it sees the white coat of the veterinary surgeon? The claws are digging into the floor and the owner looks like he is training for the World's Strongest Man competition. Well, just like Rex, the mind does not want to go there. It will resist all the way. Who can blame it? Just like the dog, it is not sure it is going to see the light of day again. However, unlike the dog, the poor old ego will not see the world again; it will become the world instead and in the process vanish like the smoke from a spent match.

See for yourself, check it out. No need to waste your money in a foreign land, though. Next time you walk down the street notice that all the houses, whatever the period, whatever the style, they all appear as this one painting, this one picture colouring consciousness this way and that. Consciousness loves to get lost here in this world of time; it is entertainment it seems. The guy pulling onto the drive in a new BMW with its out-of-the-showroom coat on appears in just the same way. The mind says the driveway and driver were here before the BMW. What nonsense!

The conventional story of objects and ageing is the inevitable outcome of thinking you exist as a separate entity. All conventionality comes with it; it is a package. There is absolutely nothing wrong with it. It is what life does. Sometimes Wholeness plays at being a someone; sometimes it does not. Ultimately, there is only ever presence. This is why thinking that liberation or enlightenment should look a certain way causes great confusion. You cannot tell Wholeness what it is. Be fair, it does not know itself. This is 'not knowing', and it is the highest form of knowing there is.

Face To No Face

This section is strongly influenced by Douglas Harding and Richard Lang from *The Headless Way* website. Douglas was a philosopher and I suppose a bit of a mystic. He was well spoken, very English and incredibly engaging and gentle. His experiments are a practical way to discover absence. But the thing that stopped me in my tracks is the idea of 'Face to No Face'.

The next time you find yourself engaged in conversation in close proximity with someone, imagine what they might see. The answer I hope you come up with is the face *you* see when you are looking in the mirror. Conversely, from your perspective, you see the face *he* sees when looking in a mirror; you are wearing each other's face. His face is appearing in your consciousness. Consciousness is appearing as his face. You have every wrinkle, every blemish and every grey hair. You have the colour of his eyes and the colour of his skin. He is so close to you it is impossible to shake him off. You have taken on his appearance.

I am going to stick my neck out here and bet you do not feel like what you look like. I would say from your perspective you feel different to what your friend has got as his experience of you. Which do you prefer? Douglas would say you are capacity for the other person. Your emptiness allows for total fullness. Try as you might, you will not stop anything colouring your blank canvas. This is a good description of unconditional love: everything is allowed to be just what it is without restriction or regulation. It is all accepted.

This, if you rest with it, is jaw-dropping stuff. No longer are you just this small monkey-like creature walking around on two legs on a planet in a galaxy, in a universe. No, whatever shows up is in you and as you. Not the person 'you'. I am using *you* as another way of saying experiencing or knowing.

This has always been the case, nothing new has happened. If you are not an object but capacity only, then you are not locatable in space or time. If you were findable you would have a boundary, an edge somewhere. There would be somewhere where you were not. Try and find this edge. If you could find an edge, then what has found this edge? May I suggest— *edgelessness*? Can you see how futile it is looking for yourself? Whatever you find is only another apparent object. This is precisely where the mind cannot go. It will try for you, I promise. But armed with what I have just written, give it a day off, will ya? Let it help with the new patio or the decorating. It is good at that; it will enjoy planning the colour scheme and working out how many rolls of paper you need. You will be surprised how sharp it is when not burdened with past and future and maintaining a spook's lifestyle.

In one of my favourite pieces, Douglas describes how, when we are young, we are told we are the image in the mirror and before too long we take this idea on board as our identity. He describes how this image locked behind glass escapes its enclosure, enters the body and turns around to look out on the world. This is the image we carry with us. This is what we imagine others see and if we are told our appearance is not up to much, we can carry around a very unlovable person for the rest of our lives.

I want to add something of my own here as well. The image we think others see is also an image of unworthiness and faults, an image that is coloured with all our past failings and thoughts about who we think we are. It is not just a physical image. There is a feeling and belief of being transparent to others and an unverified notion of the other person having access to this inner world of dread and fear. Walking around with this beast attached to you all the time, anxiety and depression are never far away. There is a sense you can never really relax in another's company. There is a fear they will rumble what you are really like, and that is what we guard with the utmost vigilance. You never get a day off. This is exhausting and debilitating. Life becomes hell and there is the wish for no more tomorrows or the next day.

Not a great picture, hey! Not everyone feels like this I guess, but it was pretty much my experience for about 40 years. Now you can appreciate what it felt like to not be what I thought I was. It's like the idea of wearing tight shoes all the time and after a while not realising they are hurting your feet. You just get used to it and put up with them. When you get the chance to take them off, the relief is immediately apparent. You can wiggle your toes again and let them out of their enclosure at last. It is just like that: feeling oneself to be in the body with the world outside. The release is like letting the air out of a balloon that has been expanding for 40 years inside your stomach. When that air goes, the relaxation is almost worthy of the contraction. The lengths Wholeness goes to notice itself. However, there is no-one to feel bitter and twisted at the last 40 years or so. There is just resting in not knowing and full-on aliveness. Everything is how it should be; nothing could have been any different. You cannot have someone else's dream; it will not work.

You may find tasks that you may have had to get a man in to do before you now tackle yourself with a new ease and confidence. I repaired my van when the immobiliser shut down the fuel pump. This saved me a packet and I can confirm it is still running today in 2012. Of course Wholeness breaks vans and also repairs them. There is no van really, but I still need it to ferry me around when I sort people's locks out.

The Appeal to Perfection

This false sense of self that is created to negotiate with the outside world can have some very high standards for itself. Because it is false it bears very little relation to what you really are. But because it imagines other people more competent than you, better looking than you and more intelligent, it seems to create an idealised image based on a fantasy of what you should be like to feel ok in the world. That idealised image will not let you win because it will always move the goal posts. No matter what you achieve, someone else will always be better at things than you are. It does not matter how much praise you receive, you do not feel that good about your achievements. It can even get to the stage you will feel embarrassed if your shoe laces come undone. It is not a case of simply stopping and retying them. You get frustrated first and only stop when the coast is clear. You have strayed from the path of perfection you laid down for yourself. This will always confirm your unworthiness to this imposter of an image. Thank goodness you are not that one. That one is a sad and doomed fellow, only suitable for the trash can.

I am probably being a bit extreme with the shoe laces, but the perfection trap can stop us from trying new things and prevent us from enjoying the company of others, because not only do we want to know everything, we want to be the best conversationalist as well. Any silences in our performance can activate the 'I am a bore' routine and then avoid any situation where you know performance may be below standard. You can never have a day off, ever.

Science: Tripping Over Its Own Shoe Laces

Scientific enquiry has shaped the world we find ourselves in today. For instance, the sophisticated communication devices that we use every day are a far cry from drums or burning beacons on hill tops.

Science describes the universe from information retrieved from painstaking experiments and deduction in association with instruments that display predictable qualities regardless of the operator: a telescope magnifies consistently, whoever it is looking through the lens.

I remember chemistry lessons at high school that described the atom and its bonding characteristics which form all the amazing bits and pieces that surround us. I would be still trying to get my head around subatomic particles and the teacher had moved on, leaving me unable to fully grasp any further information. There was a sense, somewhere, I think, that this information was more than its surface structure and had the potential to tell us something else. I wouldn't have described it in these terms then, I would just have considered myself stupid for not understanding the detailed description of why some atoms are more active than others.

The scientific account of nature renders the notion of a separate 'you' looking at the world as fantasy rather than fact. If everything in the universe can be reduced to atoms, subatomic particles and — ultimately — energy, then this account rules out actual chemistry teachers, schools and pupils. If we are being scientific, the world is therefore one homogenous blob that shapes itself into a colossal amount of variation over time, but retains the building blocks that make it up. One only has to consider the water cycle taught at junior school to appreciate that nothing dies, it just changes form over and over again. So is the sun the puddle's tormenter and eventual killer or is it its transport to join other puddles in one hell of a cloud party? If we get attached to the puddle, splash in it every day and give it a name, we'll recoil in horror on a hot day when the sunny grim reaper comes to call and takes away the best friend we'd ever had.

So it could be said that all science is based on attempts to gain more accuracy and detachment from human hopes, wishes and myths about how things are. But it is not that straightforward. Let us take the brain for example. Research has established it as one of the most complex structures the universe has pulled out of the bag. We only have to look at the billions of neurons and the neural connectivity to appreciate the permutations and patterns possible. When I studied psychology we looked at how a neuron becomes active and sends a signal to another one. Along with other neurons firing at different rates, whole areas of the brain were alive with activity. The details are complex and beyond the scope of this section: simply, the characteristics of raw materials found in nature, such as calcium, sodium and potassium, are being used to underpin the activity of the brain.

Where is the brain without this activity? Can we sensibly consider the brain on one side of the equation and the activity somewhere else? It does not make sense when looked at in this way, and yet we make the brain into an object, giving power to the noun over and above what is actually occurring; language is creating non-existent separate entities. It is so easy to get convinced and taken in by this trick because language has great power when we make the assumption that it describes a real world out there.

I suggest that it is more the case that Wholeness can do braining in the same way it can do rivering and mountaining. And here's the even more curious thing: braining is not separate from what it creates. You do not get rivers and mountains without the electrical activity of the brain. And yet, this assumption that the object is real, independent and 'out there', and the brain is representing the world 'in here' for a 'you' or a 'me' to see it and interact with it somehow, is clearly false. If we pause for a moment we see that is just not possible. Everything is too *alive* to be pigeonholed in this way. Current activity is all there is, even if memories are appearing that appeal to times and places other than the one right here.

If this is grasped, language that talks about me and you and past and future has been exposed. It is nothing other than current activity: a timeless, unceasing energy that has no beginning and no end. The mind we talk about in our everyday conversations is no longer housed within the skull of a separately existing thing we call human. No, it is demoted or promoted, whichever way you want to understand it, to an expression of life itself. Gone is the notion of birth and death, and in come drying puddles, cloud formations and rainy days filling those little hollows once again.

Apparent personal lives appear like clouds: they form, hang around for a moment with a short display and then appear invisible. The cloud has not gone anywhere because it never existed; life appeared cloudy for a while and now it is appearing as blue sky. This is Wholeness at work appearing different and maintaining itself at the same time. The consensus view of reality will not allow this formulation to take root, simply because one cannot maintain personal identity and Wholeness at the same time. Like the lucid dream described earlier on, once the dream is seen for what it is, it simply fades away.

There is no need to place science on trial for conspiracy, though. Science is an activity like everything else. I quite like computer technology, motor cars and anaesthetic while my leg is being removed; it feels good. Science has removed many diseases that would have claimed lives years ago. We have running water and electric light. But comfort is not your comfort or my comfort; it is just comfort for no one. Wholeness seems to prefer comfort over discomfort, but creates both to form a contrast.

We feel that everything that is happening is happening to a 'me'. There is not just depression; there is my depression. There is not just money; there is my money, and so on. Trying to own something and make it 'mine' is a product of seeming individuality. It cannot be avoided. It is what happens along the way and causes joy and grief as a result. However, at some level there is a feeling of disquiet and loss. Worldly activities become a symptom of something else. Like Freud's formulation of unconscious forces which shape observable behaviour without consent, this constant longing for something else is a longing to come home. It is not a negation of the world and a desire to reside in a cave on top of a mountain; it is the feeling of belonging we want. Wholeness wants to recognise itself in everything, not in quiet contemplation on a cushion somewhere. It wants to look at creation and see novelty without separation. It wants to see difference without isolation.

The apparent creation of solid, separate objects will eventually turn out to be more than a person can bear, and so collapse is inevitable. It will be at 'physical death' like the little puddle, or when the puddle realises it is made out of water and cloud and rests in everything for eternity.

Abstraction and Concepts

Do you remember your English lessons at school where you started to deconstruct language into verbs, adjectives and nouns, etc? Nouns, we were told, refer to things — objects. They form the subject of our sentences and tell us who did what to whom: 'John threw the ball' seems straightforward enough and we can, without much difficulty, identify the actor, the action and the receiver of the action.

However, our sentences can also contain nouns that do not refer to anything we can touch, smell, taste, see or hear. I am thinking about abstract nouns. Justice, love, hope, fear and time can fit into this classification nicely. We can talk about these things over dinner and engage with them through the themes of our favourite novels, but we cannot taste them the same way we can our food or drink. Food and drink, we are told, are tangible — they have a reality to them; time and love do not — they are intangible. A nice, neat division it would seem: some things are concrete; some things are ideas. Ideas are not present in the same way a body or planet Earth seem to be.

The reason I mention this is not to tell you something you already *think* you know; it is to challenge this division, this common sense notion that objects exist independently and 'out there' for all to see, but abstract ideas have to be brought to life through discussion and debate.

Objects have no more reality to them than time, love and justice do: they are all abstractions—none are present. Let me try to elaborate a bit. I am just about to press the plunger down on my coffee pot and pour the first one of the day into my favourite green mug. What could be more real and concrete than that? But none of these objects exist in the form I am giving them. I am simplifying and editing that which is infinite into a few labels that enable me to describe to you through these words an everyday activity that you may also find yourself doing from time to time. There is one scene—and I am being picky as to what I say is happening. There is no final version that can be reduced down to coffee making; coffee making is an abstraction. There is no coffee making separate from experiencing. Experiencing is appearing to be 'that'. No separation. Coffee making is an interpretation. The mind is slapping labels again, placing Post-It notes on experience so that it can know and predict.

All that seems to be happening is that stories are appearing to make sense of the infinite that has no time, edge or location. I am spinning yarns to entertain myself and my audience. This is no different from making objects out of cloud formation or believing the Plough constellation to be a real farming implement turning over the clod made out of star dust when night-time comes. The mind, or thought, is doing exactly what it is meant to do: it is creating patterns and joining up the dots.

So, I am saying that abstraction and storytelling are essentially the same thing. Calling a 'cup' a cup is no problem. It can form part of our narrative when we tell someone about our favourite one or how we dropped Grandma's antique one when a child and being slapped for our carelessness. Storytelling is entertaining; there is a kind of magic to it.

But storytelling is a 'happening', a current activity. The ideas for our stories appear presently and colour consciousness this way and that. The same editing goes on when we describe the vicissitudes of our love life to our best friend or the way people we know appear to us over time. It is as if the moment we start to talk and think we are adding a chapter to the epic we call 'me and my life'.

This is why as soon as we start to talk about non-duality it becomes fantasy. We know it's fantasy because 'reality' cannot be talked about directly: there is nothing to talk about. All the words you may hear at a satsang or meeting point to something that cannot be grasped and cannot be pinned down. If you have been to a few meetings or watched YouTube videos of people asking questions, you will notice and feel the frustration of the 'spiritual' seeker trying to fit what is being suggested into a familiar framework that underpins our day-to-day stories. Time, purpose and logic appear over and over again. You will not get this; you cannot take it home with you and display it on your mantelpiece.

This is excellent news, however. If you understood It, you would be someone understanding something. You are back to square one. Not knowing is another way of pointing to seamless Wholeness. Not knowing is what's left when stories are seen as stories. Not knowing is peace. Not knowing is constant wonderment. Not knowing can't be known. Not knowing *is*.

Unlike abstraction and stories, experiencing or being need absolutely nothing. You cannot embellish being to make it look more attractive and more exciting; you've got diddlysquat to work with. It is already complete as this timelessness right here, right now. Can you see why 'unconditional love' is a term that is used frequently? Being asks for nothing and gives everything. You can never leave yourself; yourself can never leave you. There are no parts and no pieces. Prior to appearances — you are, and with appearances — you are. If that's not pointing to completeness and oneness for you, then you are very hard to please. When Wholeness 'sees' itself it realises it 'cannot' see itself; it *is* itself. Silence and stillness in the form of calamity and farce continue to dance around. The court jester we call our life continues to entertain and amuse. We can still cry, we can still smile, and we can still get angry. Aliveness will not be tamed by stories. Aliveness appears *as* stories. There is no story that will be the end of all stories. Stories are the beginning, the middle and the end of everything.

Nothing needs to be any different to what already is. It is when fantasy seduces us that life can become serious business. Believing that there really are people outside of us, encircling us, placing us in the middle and taunting us, is the stuff of nightmares and dreams. Row after row of other faces, other bodies and other voices gnaw at us constantly. Some throw abuse; others throw sticks and stones. Their eyes seem to pierce our soul. They can see our filthy core. We will never live up to the standard they demand because they will shift the goalposts and reserve their praise for tomorrow or the next day. We try to please and bargain for some respite. We may be granted the odd concession and life may look a little rosier. But remember, roses have their thorns as well. Do not be fooled by the sweet smell of victory: thorns and brambles are never far away to tangle and trip us.

The point I am making is that abstraction and story-telling can take hold to such an extent they can drown us and suck the lifeblood out of us, leaving just the shrivelled skin and empty husk. Timeless being trumps all stories, all fantasy.

The good news is that we can still edit by adding and deleting and make up all sorts of stories. We can believe we were born, we can believe that we will die. We can shake hands with someone, hug, kiss and love them with all our heart. Nothing needs to be any different.

To kiss another person's lips is to kiss our own. To shake another's hand is to shake our own. We are only ever experiencing ourselves through everything life throws at us. We can stop pretending; stop believing we're someone or something. We have played our game and made our point. Suffering and confusion can wake us up in the same way falling from a great height in a dream can. We will never hit the ground in a dream and we will never reach the base of a bottomless pit. Once we see there is only dream, the impact of a 'me' having a life becomes as ridiculous as the impact from the bottomless pit. We can pull ourselves together — there's no need to pull ourselves apart!

Reading what has been written about abstraction and concepts and socially constructed meanings can be mighty difficult to grasp if we only know and accept what we have been taught about life, the universe and everything. The so-called solid world is perhaps too solid and real to be questioned. The hypnotic spell is taking a long while to wear off. A click of the fingers to be 'back in the room' does not seem to work for us. I am going to look at hypnotism in the next chapter, simply because it deserves a good seeing to. I want to end this one, though, with how I see the process of abstraction and the formulation of concepts.

Have you seen the television programme *How It's Made*? They take everyday objects, such as a drink can or a musical instrument, and show you from start to finish the various processes that go into producing it from raw materials at one end to a recognisable, fully functioning thing at the other. Imagine you are in a trumpet factory producing high quality instruments for professional musicians. You are watching the production line where various people perform different tasks and assemble separate pieces, ready to send it on to the next guy down the line. You watch as the brass gets rolled and shaped by the metal worker, hammering and soldering the seams to an invisible airtight seal. Tubes get bent and valves sit nicely into holes. Heating and polishing ensure durability and attractiveness, and the guy has a blow and a press to test-drive the birth of a new addition to the family. Finally, it gets wrapped and boxed and labelled as 'trumpet'.

Now, abstraction is the same kind of process as the one described above. Let us take something not man -made, say a flower, a rose, maybe. If you could observe one right now you might notice its stem and its leaves. You can feel the thorns and smell the aroma. Count the petals and notice those central projections we call stamens that produce pollen at the tip, and we are well on our way to describing the rose. If thought is our factory production line, then we have taken the raw materials, in this case the noticed parts, the visible parts, of the flower, and stuck them together through investigation and knowledge. The parts have been processed. We have selected some parts over others. But, just as with the trumpet, there is no flowerness or trumpetness there which is above and beyond the entire process of mental model building and labelling. Look at it this way: if the trumpet went out of fashion and orders were down, the factory could start making fancy brass funnels out of the end piece of the trumpet. Similar processes could take place to produce it, it would just be quicker and a new label would be printed saying 'brass funnels'. The same brass is functioning differently. There is no trumpet or funnel that can be labelled once and for all. For those of you in a pedantic mood there is no brass either: brass is an alloy of zinc and copper.

Similarly, the thing we call 'rose' might simply be regarded as a natural device for making petals, whose only use is to scent water for special ceremonies and rituals on the fourth Sunday of every month in a leap year. Roses would therefore be non-existent: they have no function other than to make petals for a sacrament. Sending a single red rose to a loved one might be considered offensive, or even blasphemous.

So concepts are the result of mental abstraction and not the depiction of a solid, preformed, pre-existing and unchanging world out there, to be observed and recorded for all time. If you are brave enough, look at the body and the self in the same way. The mind may resist this kind of exploration; just give it a slap and tell it to listen for once. I will leave you to explore this on your own without any of my ideas contaminating you. All I will say is this: if you come up with anything interesting, discard it and start again.

My take on things, as you will realise, is to look for yourself, feel for yourself and stop hanging on to a guru, master or celebrity spiritual teacher. They are all a load of pants, and rightly so. I am not being disparaging here; I am just alerting you to the fact that you are the sole authority on yourself and not the ideas from fictitious characters in a book or film. Paying more money to sit closer to a famous teacher is just unnecessary. Mind you, you won't listen to me or my load of pants either. Your dream is your dream. Just because I didn't go to meetings does not mean you shouldn't. That bolt of lightning might strike you — who knows? In some ways writing down these words will always be my take on things and I won't pretend it isn't.

Look Into My Eyes

Don't forget, we are still in the pub, you and me, and the red leather seats are warming up nicely. The snow is still falling and the ale is still flowing.

'Another plate of strong cheese and fresh crusty bread, please, barman!'

'I want you to simply relax and concentrate on my voice. Look into my eyes, and allow yourself to trust me completely, unquestionably and wholeheartedly... You're under.'

'Everything I say from now on you are to believe and not doubt a single word: you are a separate entity that was born in the past and will die in the future. You live on a planet we call 'Earth'. You exist with other people similar to you. There is something called 'time' that will ensure your progress through life as you reach your goal and realise your purpose. The goal is... '

'3-2-1, you're back in the room.'

We are all familiar with hypnosis, both as a form of therapy to rid us of phobias or to arrest our unhealthy eating habits, and as entertainment in a stage show that can highlight how suggestible and gullible we can be.

I remember, whilst on holiday with my brother, we witnessed a stage hypnotist convince a young woman there was a fairy only a few inches tall dancing and singing right in front of her. The woman had been convinced that this Tinkerbell was the most magical and kindest fairy that had ever lived. In fact Tinkerbell was the best friend she'd ever had. The joy and love in her eyes was amazing to see and there was no doubt some message had been implanted into her brain. The real test was when my brother walked on stage and squashed poor Tinkerbell dead. Of course, the hypnotist orchestrated this manoeuvre and so it was all part of the act. Watching this woman slap my brother so hard around the face, though, raised an almighty laugh from the audience and a sense of amazement from me that anyone can be convinced of something so supernatural.

Well, if you subscribe to the view about birth, death, planets and time, you are also under a spell. You are asleep. You are dreaming. You are totally immersed in the drama you call 'me and my life'. Just like the woman watching her beloved Tinkerbell, you have taken on board a view of life that is bogus and fragmented. A life that you have been convinced that you *have*, that you own. Parents, teachers and peers, in fact the entire back catalogue of human history is weaving its magic and showing us how to see and what to see. There is a consensus reality of objects and perceivers that colour our every thought, our every action, and reaction. The world is out there and obvious. You are seeing it and interacting with it. It is full of peril. It is full of danger. You have got to make it work because you have a life and you better look after it. You had better play the game and play it well. Sit up straight, stop slouching. Eat your dinner and be grateful you are not poor and starving. Love your parents and respect your elders and those of higher status and class.

Enjoy education; it is for your own good. Learn about the world and learn about your place in the cosmos and in the scheme of things. Play your role: you are a man, a woman; you are English or African; you are a Buddhist or a Christian. Save the whale but abuse your spouse. Be 'good' in this life and gloat in the next. Progress is good, we are going somewhere. Tomorrow things will be better.

I will stop there because you are probably running out of breath. I have told it like this to give the sense of absolute frenetic activity and railroad expectations. Unceasing and unrelenting *doing* and becoming appear to be so commonplace. For most it appears there is no problem with 'normality'. We accept we were born and had a beginning, and we accept, probably with degrees of fear and imagination, our eventual demise. Some of us think that we will leave this world behind to continue somewhere else, a 'better place', with the secret laid at our feet and the satisfaction we have done well.

Many people, it seems, have accepted life as it is presented to them from a very young age by those who genuinely want us to function well and play the same game everyone is playing and not appear out of place, or, even worse, mad, bad or a total misfit. We become socialised and hypnotised. In short, we are conditioned.

Conditioning reminds me of Pavlov's dogs. If you are not familiar with this, I will explain. Pavlov was a Russian physiologist working in the late nineteenth and early twentieth century. He was interested in the digestive system and performed experiments on animals. He wired them up and studied their digestive chemicals, how they are produced and how they function. Whilst studying dogs and the salivation associated with feeding times, he noticed that even before the food was presented, the dog salivated at the seeing of the white coat of the experimenter. The dog had made a connection between 'white coat' and 'dinner time'. The dog was behaving based on future predictions. In a way, a kind of mental world that paired an everyday neutral event with a reward was operating at some level for the animal.

Are we much different? As babies our rudimentary gurgles and babblings are greatly shaped by reinforcement in the wake of intonation and praise from an adult who tries to get baby to say 'car'. At first, a just noticeable 'C' might be all that is needed for a smile and hug from Mum or Dad. You can see that over time a pattern of light that resembles the object we regularly receive a hug for, might result in a pointy finger and a clear reciting of 'car'. Hand claps and praise, 'clever little boy', stand in for a plate of butcher's tripe and a Bonio biscuit.

This, to me, is the beginning of hypnosis. The stage hypnotist does his warm-up routine in half an hour to select a suitable victim; education in 'humans' takes a little longer. Once achieved, though, it is a devil to extinguish. If only we could be reassured by a life hypnotist for being a wonderful participant and that we will remember nothing of the evening. We could walk into reality like walking back to our seat. A round of applause and a ribbing from our witnesses might be all that is needed for us to stop pretending. I am saying this, but if it is seen for what it is, then nothing needs to change and nothing needs to alter. You are already one hell of a miracle. Believing you are a farmyard chicken clucking your head off is nothing to what there is on a day-to-day basis. Taking a look at your own hands now and again and saying to yourself, "What on earth are these?" is enough to break the spell. You never made them; they just appear, like the morning sunshine and the evening moonlight.

Creating the Drama

If you have experienced the relief of waking from a bad dream, you will know how it feels *not* to have actually lost a loved one or perhaps not to have actually murdered someone and not actually have the police hot on your trail. On waking, you can rest assured that what you thought was real was only fantasy and imagination. Phew!

This chapter will explore the possibility of that 'phew' happening right here, right now in the so-called waking state. Just as in the dream, the apparent everyday life of relationships, jobs, birth and death is a creation, a fantasy — a fabrication. It belongs just as much to the thoughts and ideas of those that precede you as it does to you, the person reading this now. It is all made-up. None of it is happening. It is all dream appearance. 'You' do not 'have' a mother, father, brother or sister. There is no outside world full of animals, mountains and weather systems.

No. Thinking is concocting the whole shebang. Nothing, but nothing, exists outside of thought. Concepts are handed down to us to reduce the fear of the unknown, both for the benefactor and the recipient. You are being handed a baton by those already on the move. Grasp it and run! Round and round you go chasing, chasing and chasing. You can pass it on if you like — it might just ease the burden — or drop it and exit the race. What you think of as an external world is 'thinking' doing what it does best: creating stories, or — more colloquially — bullshitting!

I want to take a look at this bullshitting to see how it starts; its function; why it can create fear of a world; and — more importantly — why it can lead to anxiety and the fear of other people.

To assist us, I am going to create an analogy using a cinema screen and the curtains. The curtains seem to obscure the screen and so control how much light is on view. The screen is representing timeless being and the curtains can be thought of as internal mental structures built from very early experiences. Some lives seem to exist with the curtains tightly shut and others have them drawn back to differing degrees, creating various openings and life experiences. The curtains, or mental structures, only appear to block out light. Whatever you think is happening, and no matter whether you have a love story, horror movie or comedy, the light is always burning as brightly as ever behind the scenes; you only have to turn around and see. The drama itself seems hypnotising and serious, but it is the light that illuminates all scripts, all acts and all scenes. It not only illuminates; it appears in and as every picture.

We will return to the analogy later. I just wanted you to have a feel of it before I continue.

As children it appears we are born into a pre-existing world full of meaning established by our predecessors and maintained now by the ones who are in our immediate proximity. You are a thing that is being cared for by another thing. After a while the novelty of a sweet little darling with little human features wears off: 'You, young man, have to fit in with us! Not the other way around. Understand?'

We cannot have all we want. All our needs will never be met, even by the most attentive and loving parents. There will be times when we are not fed quickly enough or when we just feel uncomfortable in this strange new world not of our making. We cannot be satisfied. The world has become inadequate and scary.

Now, rather than there be just timeless being, Wholeness goes — 'zshoom', retreats, and closes some very hefty iron-studded double doors. Behind these doors there is a hive of activity, an activity that the remaining light you call 'me' is totally oblivious to. It's unconscious and out of awareness. The curtains either side of the auditorium have almost closed and are concealing a factory. This factory is where people are made and an outside world constructed. This is your 'birth', not the parturition we normally associate with human beginnings. This is the birth of the individual!

Well, thank heavens it's not real. However, you don't know that yet. It seems the drama that unfolds is your riddle to solve. Solve it, and like Indiana Jones rearranging those stone tablets at the foot of an ancient temple, the door opens. You find the treasure.

But let's not get ahead of ourselves. I can see I am spoiling it by giving away the plot.

The world that appears as a result of Wholeness contracting is the one with which we seem to interact. This is the world of independently existing separate objects and separately existing others. This is the world. This is the drama.

Wholeness is convinced, now, it is something; it exists in relationship to the outside world. There is a me here and a you there. Now there is a striving to get along, to be considerate of each other's feelings and have respect for one another. We establish roles. We have identities to maintain. I am a son with you, a dad with you, a brother with you and a very sexy body with you.

This mental factory turns out purpose, meaning, history, time, duty and — above all — guilt! You are not good enough. You will never be a patch on the idealised version of you that appears the same time the 'bad bastard' does. The idealised self is what is sought. Almost all behaviour directed toward ourselves and to others takes its inspiration from this image of perfection. There is an enormous compulsion to realise the idealised self through activities that seem to show the constructed external world that we are doing really well and are a very successful human being. The persona or mask we wear, though, hides a secret of a mild feeling of something missing or the extremes of madness, badness and a strong sense of worthlessness. It will never occur to the seeker that the idealised self is unobtainable. It is as elusive as the pot of gold at the end of the rainbow.

The idealised self is based on hope. It is based on future attainment and good deeds done. It is the kind of self you imagine will please others. Other people will surely like you and you will fit in nicely with their plans and aspirations. You will make people laugh and be the life and soul of the party. The compulsion to please others is to externalise your sense of self.

There is always a looking in the wrong direction for decision making and right action. You will find nothing of any use in a barren land like this. Nothing grows there. The environmental conditions do not allow it. If you continue to till this soil you will end up with a dust bowl and a total blindness when the wind whips up a storm of dust that only obscures and confuses. The real self, if there is such a thing, does not look to anyone for security or comfort. It's always been here; you don't need to look for it. You can leave your job, leave your house, leave your spouse and kids and even leave your country, but you can never leave 'home'. Home is non-separation. Home is where the heart is.

The attempt at being good is to feed an identity behind the scenes that has one almighty appetite. Have you seen *Little Shop of Horrors*? Well, just like poor Seymour the florist, you have an Audrey II plant, requiring blood and human flesh in the form of constant self-monitoring and self-sacrifice. Seymour could not satisfy the out-of-control plant and the story ends in catastrophe.

All mental structures, like Seymour's man-eating plant/ego, are always on the brink of collapse. It is only complex mental engineering keeping them up. Without this, those structures crumple and crumble and morph into dust. A good gust of wind and they are gone — no more. This is all that is noticed at liberation. It was all a dream — no substance.

Your drama is unique; nobody else has it. There is something I heard in my search that struck a chord with me. I will attribute it to Peter Brown from www.theopendoorway.org. Where he got it from, I don't know, but it is this: 'You are the sole inhabitant of your universe' or words to that effect. Your experience is all you ever know. I can't impress on you enough the impact those words had on me. Even now, writing it down for you I feel… well, I just can't say. You'll find out for yourself one day. When you realise there is nobody here but *you* and that everything, even what you consider as other people, appears in your experience Now for ever and ever and ever. There is an energy here that dreams-up worlds, time and journeys in order to lose itself in drama. Sometimes it stops pretending and reveals itself to itself, but only when it does and only when it feels like it.

All objects that appear just appear. But they are not objects; it is you seeing yourself. The world of appearances is your reflection — not that ugly mug in the mirror. Your reflection is not that personal. It might include the image you see brushing its teeth in the morning, but exclusivity to this one will only induce pain, suffering and fear. The world of appearances points to the eternal only, not the impermanent world. How magnificent!

This has always been the case; it just became downgraded to normality. Normality is being born, having parents, getting a job, looking forward to holidays and generally fitting into a system that we have been convinced pre-dates us. Or, indeed, trying consciously to live outside the system, going off the grid, being self-sufficient and having an alternative lifestyle. The astounding recognition that life is amazing and totally mysterious is hardly noticed. The contracted self that lives in a body with a world outside believes only the constant ramblings of the internal objects constructed to alleviate the fear of not knowing and unpredictability. This is why trying to discuss 'non-duality' at a dinner party with friends just won't be heard. You might as well be speaking a foreign language. The other dramas showing on screens one, two and three are providing all the entertainment necessary for your friends and colleagues. Don't bother with subtitles either, in the form of showing them ancient teachings or introducing 'self-enquiry', the silly buggers won't read them.

The drama constructed from a fear of a dreamt separate world creates constant anxiety for a person. Your eyes are fixed on a future that never arrives. This false sense of 'me' will never be happy — ever. It thinks it knows how to be happy by emulating others who it thinks are doing well and who prosper in the world. The pursuit of physical riches and admiration is like peeking through the cracks of the stage curtains at a cold, black, white and grey audience, not noticing the constant light, colour and warmth shining constantly within you. It seems Wholeness will do absolutely anything to gain what it thinks it has lost. It will travel to holy places and seek out holy people. It will try and control thought and goes out of its way to be compassionate to others.

Wholeness may not be as stupid as you might think. The seeking keeps the drama going all the time that there is a someone looking for a future, and that 'future' includes enlightenment. If you were watching a movie and paid your money, you would be rather miffed if it ended after only ten minutes: let's face it, you have hardly had time to become irritated by the kid behind you kicking your seat, let alone start on the bucket of popcorn.

It appears that some people are mighty fortunate and have what seems to be a half-hour sitcom as their drama; other poor sods have the director's cut of War and Peace. When it's over for them, they find themselves dead in their seat and get taken straight to the crematorium, cooked in the chair they were watching from.

So, dramas are all unique. Wholeness likes to sit and watch multiple screens, flicking through the channels, laughing at some and crying with others. When it finally switches off the set, silence and stillness provide all the entertainment required. The blockbuster called 'having a life' starts to lose its appeal. It is like when you are growing-up, *Tom and Jerry* get replaced by horrors, thrillers or so-called adult entertainment. Mind you, when the false sense of separation gets rumbled *Tom and Jerry* can become an absolute scream. Watch the episode *Jerry and Jumbo*, where a baby elephant falls from the travelling circus train and ends up making friends with Jerry — hilarious.

Dramas need their sets. They need context for their plots and venues for their actors to exchange dialogue. Old westerns had the shop fronts and saloon bars propped up with timber bracing, and if you have noticed the wobble on wooden frames from slammed doors on low-budget soap operas, you will know what I mean. Clever camera crews and multiple angles show us just enough information to fool us and help us play along with the film makers.

The life drama is no different. Right now I am sitting in my office writing this close to Christmas. There is a parcel downstairs that needs taking to the local post office, a ten minute walk away. This requires imagination on a grand scale because the parcel, the post office and even the downstairs are not present. All that's happening is that pen is squiggling on paper and thought objects are creating the next scene of parcel posting.

Nothing is actually happening other than thought which is building sets and writing scripts. How absolutely amazing this is. It is so obvious when *personing* collapses and becomes impossible when Wholeness takes a world view.

I wonder sometimes what on earth the readers of this must think, especially those who have picked it up at a jumble sale or found it clearing out a relative's attic. If I'd have read this when younger it wouldn't have meant a damn thing. Non-duality seemed to drop in my lap without any warning; perhaps it will do the same for you. If it's way in the future, dear reader, goodness knows what technology you will have and what tyrants and tossers are around manipulating your thought processes and telling you how to be. All I'll say is this: timeless being does not change; there is nothing to change.

The Fear of Other People

I have touched on the fear of other people already, but this was so dominant for me that I want to look at it in more detail.

What are other people? What is another person? It seems an easy question on the surface. You could respond by saying other human beings are like myself, who, although similar in basic design, have subtle differences in body shape and intellectual abilities. Some people are older than you; some are younger. Some are richer and some are poorer.

Straightforward? No. So-called 'other people' act only as a stimulus to activate templates, mental characters or stereotypes constructed early on in our lives to make sense and protect an unstable feeling of selfhood. You never see a human being as they actually are; you are positioning yourself based on your best interpretation of them. You are attempting to read their mind and second-guess what they are capable of based on experiences from the past. Behind those closed doors of the factory other people are being assembled from parts and pieces of encounters in the past. What you are left with is a chimera constructed in a crude and very ad hoc fashion. You are Victor Frankenstein. Welcome to your monster.

Like Frankenstein's monster, your creation does you no favours. It will not be restrained, and goes on the rampage. In a sense you are both in bondage — you and your creation. To create is to destroy. What is destroyed is the uncertainty and mystery of life itself. Notions of creation leave you in bondage and thinking you know what the world is and what is happening. You can't know. You will never know. It's not possible. Knowing is the expulsion from the Garden of Eden. Ignorance is thinking you know; it isn't the common-sense notion of being stupid.

A perceived successful and confident other person can activate the loser in you. Thought can establish scenario after scenario of what 'their kind' are like. You imagine the expensive restaurants they patronise, their political ideology and even the acrobatic sexual activities in which they most probably engage. Your thought factory turns out people faster than a milk bottle being filled in a dairy. Not only that, the current person under construction is recycled for another day where bits and pieces of the current character are used for someone else we meet, perhaps years later.

How grotesque.

The mind of a separate person is often suspicious of others and on guard. To be a person is to be vulnerable and frightened. Behaviour around others is often to protect and pre-empt a strike at the fragile structure we call 'me'. To relax and just *be* is like having a defence budget of about £1.50. That's not enough to protect you from attack. You might as well wave a white hanky even before you shake hands for the first time.

It does not have to be this way. You are not seeing anything as it actually is. You are living in fantasy. To think you know what anything is, and that includes other people, is at best inaccurate and worse — totally wrong. The whole notion of there being other people is a by-product of the internal structure established to defend and make sense of a world that comes with contraction and sense-making.

Let's face it, if you are a shy and fearful person and are with a crowd of strangers you will automatically feel self-conscious. Imagine you are in a pub or a bar you haven't been to before. It might be filled with lots of laughter and lots of people who know each other very well. You might witness the bar staff exchanging words with the punters on a very informal basis and feel rather uncomfortable because you are clearly a strange face to others. It's like catching a glimpse of a movie half-way through and not knowing the characters or the plot.

When self-consciousness ceases, there are only flashes of light and sound and lots and lots of storytelling. The mind constructs scenes complete with people and places to make sense of the infinite. Boundlessness and lack of definition scare the life out of an engineered self.

I can assure you that liberation does not stop thought, though. Thought is seen as this incredible phenomenon that arises out of nothing and falls back into nothing. Like a lucid dream, it is taken to be entertainment — no different from reading a novel or going to the cinema. It has no power to do anything. It is always playing catch-up, interpreting from old knowledge and ignoring the present appearance of everything in and as this timeless realm.

If you see what I am trying to convey, you will never be bored again. The mystery of what is will be a constant travelling companion for you. So, sitting in traffic with others becoming frustrated at the one metre per minute progress will be a source of pleasure while you are look-ing at the surroundings and hearing the tutting and cuss-ing of your fellow passengers.

In liberation, the very thing seeming to be a constant cause of anxiety can morph into utter fascination and interest. Listening — real listening — where you seek clarification from another to really grasp their thoughts shows the utmost respect for someone. Rather than stored knowledge becoming activated or crass stock phrases being used, you give another the space to express them-selves. You can still misunderstand someone, however, but you seem to have the confidence to admit it, and you are intrigued and interested all the same. There is no inner structure to sway about and become unstable after an attempt to criticise you and your lack of knowledge. There is no separate person in residence to receive and interpret this. What you are becomes unbounded and free and unaffected by the neurotic needs of others.

Fear can come in all guises and so my fears are not your fears. But I think fear of other people is ubiquitous and the source of a lot of depression, anxiety and cruel vindictive behaviour designed to belittle and control oth-ers. Fear of others is not just the withdrawing from social situations so as not to be exposed as an unworthy human candidate; it can appear as always wanting to be the best around others and the withholding of praise and love if someone achieves more than you. The self which emerges from early unsatisfactory encounters with parents and teachers strives for perfection. If this perfection is clearly out of reach, the fear of being found out and having your Achilles heel on show will activate aggression as well as self-pity. It is much easier to inflict harm on others if we feel ourselves threatened and in danger.

Judging others and creating a personality for them has very little to do with who or what they are. In a way we are always writing two scripts — ours and theirs. This is inevitable and comes with the package labelled: *I am a separate person.* Not only do we imprison ourselves, we create an accomplice and share a bunk bed with him or her in jail.

Interactions are influenced by the internal drama. This is the dynamism that drives so much misery and unsatisfactory behaviour. It is as if you are a talent scout searching for someone to play a role in your production. If someone leaves you to star in, or play a supporting part in, another drama, then there is a role that needs filling. You cannot put on the performance without a cast; who would come to see that? A drama with no actors is a non-entity. It makes me wonder if it's why some people find themselves in more than one abusive relationship. They don't know it, but they are probably looking for someone to play the role of tyrant and torturer. Gaps feel uncomfortable and confusing. No identity is tantamount to death for the person. So, any identity, even that of a slave to a cruel and abusive partner, can seem better than having nothing to cling on to at all.

Shyness and anxiety do not exist independently — just like everything else. Anxiety requires created events. We can stimulate the anxious person by giving him or her a script that will suit the artistic prowess of the actor within. No actor likes being out of work and twiddling their thumbs. Anything is better than nothing and so you will make it your own and impress the director no matter what. Even if the role is exhausting and scary it shows you are still a 'someone' rather than a 'no one'. Misery doesn't necessarily cause a person to seek help, though, to find out what the problem is. There is an energy in misery and depression that can become addictive. It becomes addictive because it is predictable. If you have ever experienced depression you will know how a flat-line internal state is maintained no matter what anyone says or does. In the prison of depression, every day is much the same as the one before it. There is a pseudo sense of control over your life. The curtains are closed — private viewing only.

The anxious person was created very early on from inevitable unsatisfactory life events. It is far easier to think of ourselves as bad, mad or just plain faulty rather than our carers not being quite up to the job of looking after us. Our parents are like gods: all powerful and all knowing. The internal bad person becomes the villain in our production, dressed in a dark cloak and lurking in the shadows down a dark alley somewhere. But like all mental structures, it needs feeding and nurturing through suitable scripts that show it off: Vincent Price and Boris Karloff didn't do many love stories; they were cast as monsters and mad scientists, not lovers departing on trains going in opposite directions.

An identity emerges to manage the world that was apparently created by separation. Thought becomes our world because independent objects do not exist. A world pushed outside by the mind/brain is based on the past and the ideas created by a naïve young child from way back. We only ever see our own ideas and beliefs about what we think exists, but because we are essentially split, with many voices and many objects clamouring for recognition and expression, we can believe thoughts as reality and adjust our behaviour accordingly.

This is what is meant by living in a closed loop; we are just not open to seeing without expectation and are always trying to gain something to fill the gulf left by turning our back on ourself. Of course I mean turning our back on Wholeness, not *you* the imposter who thinks s/he exists and will die. The person that emerges from a primordial state of undifferentiating and timelessness masquerading as a thing, a *me*, can be anxious, aggressive, competitive, withdrawn or anything else that makes for a good play. The relinquishing of this thing is a kind of death. It is surely amazing how the mind-made structure that entertains and plagues us in equal measure will not succumb to logic or reasoning. Although, to be fair, if an identity is created that seems to run the show, it's no surprise there is a clinging to it. Letting go would be like having your own child dangling over a cliff with your hands firmly attached to their wrists. Who would allow themselves to release them just because some guy says he's young and will probably bounce his way to safety? It won't happen.

This is why perceived 'death' can be the driving force behind most of our thoughts and actions. To die, we think, is to lose an identity, something that has been with us right from day one. This has become so precious because it is all we think we are and all we think we have. Take that away and where am I? This is why if therapy only works with fixing this *me* it is doomed from the start. (I will talk about counselling and psychotherapy later. I've been on both sides in the counselling room and so offer you my thoughts on it.)

New situations and novel events when a person is operating as a contracted independent *me* are totally false. Novelty and new will be seen only when the person has packed his bags and disappeared. So-called new events such as an invite to a party or a job interview are not unique for the me. The drama within is constructing a scary story to feed this pathetic creature made from the past. Thought anticipates how the me will perform in the interview or at the party. We are sure what your interviewers or other guests will be like. The heart will beat faster weeks beforehand as a response to a thought object appearing in scene four, act three of an apparent life. When we finally pull our body to the actual interview or put our best clothes on for the party, we can be consumed by negative thoughts and be everywhere except enjoying the party or answering the job-related questions. This is precisely what I mean by fantasy and imagination. This is what a drives a separate person. This is what can cease. The drama can end. What is left is sheer entertainment. Is there a difference between entertainment and drama?

Find out!

A Person Can Only Seek

There is only Wholeness — nothing else. The creation of personhood is Wholeness turning its back on itself and creating a structure to deal with an alien universe it has created for itself. Wholeness never leaves itself and never stops being whole. A kind of hypnosis, in the form of time, purpose and meaning, fuels the search for some kind of future glory — to be wonderful, successful and loveable.

This ignorance is all that falls away. Ignorance is ego. It is a loss that is felt at liberation, not a gain. You are left raw and naked with nothing to pull you or push you anymore. There is a relaxation and resting that cannot be described and cannot be given or worked for. The curtains of the cinema screen are drawn all the way back with nothing obscuring the screen. You can see the whole lot. The curtains were concealing the factory door whose inner workings were responsible for the drama that gripped you all your life. Once you had only the version of life the factory produced. It turns out the quality control was shit — letting things go out that belonged in the rubbish bin and not for your consumption.

The 'me', the individual, is the search. All the time there is trying to find something in particular it is growing and growing and growing. Audrey II has an insatiable appetite. Feed it and it will only end in tears.

A glimpse is a chink of light leaking through a faint gap in the curtains. The chink may intensify the search, allowing the me to come up with all sorts of rubbish which explains an alteration in reality whilst reading a spiritual book or sitting in a 'meeting with friends'. This for me was the most uncomfortable period of my entire life. Locked away in my study, watching hour after hour of videos and listening to hundreds of audio files, was like being possessed by a demon. I locked my family out of my life so as to endure the sensation of being ripped from limb to limb on my own and in total privacy.

I know I am being dramatic here, but that's how it was for me. It was horrendous. It wasn't nice and blissful. On the flip side, what could be called liberation or integration was hardly noticed. It was more like saying: 'Oh, my word. This is it. Well, who'd have thought?'

Therapy: Being Honest

Not many non-dual writings give much space for counselling and psychotherapy, and so I can sense the advaita police polishing their handcuffs as I start to write. I can see why. Therapy tends to be all about an individual discovering something, understanding their past and moving on in life.

I want to look at therapy as the breaking through of honesty and the falling away of knowing and certainty. I have had various forms of therapy over the last ten years or so and I studied the rationale of therapies when I was exploring psychology with The Open University.

In my experience it is one thing to be knowledgeable about different kinds of therapy and quite another to admit one's own vulnerability. You realise and accept you are not coping very well, and find yourself sitting next to a stranger who you think might be able to fix you. You look around at the certificates on the wall and the Kleenex on the table — scary stuff. I'll tell you this much, though: if you get this far you have done well, regardless of the final outcome.

I can remember picking up the phone and making an appointment, and, my word, there was some activity in my chest area before my call was answered. It's weird because when I found myself sitting there in the room with a 'professional' I felt like a fraud: I was fine really; I had made a mistake. For me, there was also a feeling I had to produce something; I had to show the therapist the thing she could help me with.

After a period of silence where there was a lot of selection and internal rehearsal, my mouth opened and I spoke. My first words were: "I am so unhappy." Not that ground-breaking, I know, but for me that was the first piece of real gut-reaching honesty I had ever verbalised in my entire life.

The weeks rolled by and I talked and I talked. A valve had been opened and I was talking about things that escaped the internal censor that had worked incredibly well in the past. This isn't the book to go into much detail about the revelations in therapy. However, the point of this chapter is the link with non-duality, and it is simply this — honesty.

Real honesty is an absence, an absence of pretending and bluffing. It is admitting you are not alright and you are not managing. For me, the input from the therapist was beside the point; it was the staring at some demon squarely in the face and not backing down that had the real power.

To me this was *The Gunfight at the Non-Dual Corral*. It was years later when non-duality raised its head that I faced myself again — the rematch if you like. I am sure it was honesty that was operating on that November day outside the supermarket: I admitted to myself, I did not know what I was looking at or what was going on. There was only total mystery.

Honesty, to me, is a letting go of certainty and knowing what something is. Honesty is saying you don't understand when someone is trying to describe some-thing technical to you. Dishonesty is falsely nodding your head when someone is showing you how to use the latest software or explaining some scientific theory. It is the perfection trap opening up ready to swallow you if you own up to uncertainty.

The paradox is that uncertainty is liberating; think-ing you know what anything is means bondage and suf-fering. Knowledge can be such a bind and a barrier to the simple joys in life, like enjoying another's company. In not knowing, a conversation with someone is truly amazing because you no longer know what is happening. Of course you never did; you just thought you did.

Honesty, for me, is another word for Wholeness and timelessness. In honesty you admit that no recognisable objects appear in your absence — not a thought, not an apple, not a pyramid and not another person. An object cannot be separate from experiencing or aliveness. An object is the formless in form, timelessness as an idea of time. They define each other and appear together — not apart. You cannot envisage a mountain without a valley or left without right. There simply is what there is. Honesty is recognising the mind as one hell of an entertainer who can do drama, horror, love stories and comedy.

Throw your television away. Noticing the bullshit that used to pass as reality will provide all the entertain-ment you will ever need. Listening to a friend pour out their heart about a partner's infidelity may still activate the customary, 'Oh, how dreadful. What a selfish bastard!' But at the same time there is an absolute knowing that boyfriends appear in dreams. Sometimes they are faith-ful, sometimes they feel the urge to play hide the salami with anyone who shows the slightest bit of interest.

The awesome power of mind as a dot-to-dot artist is seen for what it is — a story maker. In a way you acquire new skills of playing along so as to provide credibility to your friend's awful life. It would be totally inappropriate to trot out some non-dual statement that "all there is is Wholeness, so get over it!"

So therapy stopped the lies; it didn't fix Richard Bates. Richard Bates was rumbled and dissolved. He never felt better about himself: he reached out to 'daddy' and was never seen again.

I hope the non-dual purists and law enforcement will let me off with a warning for mentioning therapy. I'll settle for a clip across the ear. Sorry!

Before I move on to something else, there is one more thing I want to mention about therapy, and this arose only in the last twelve months.

I enrolled on a counselling course at my local college and thought I might give it a go. I did have reservations, especially after the non-dual stuff, but I went anyway. I was already familiar with the theory side of things and found myself helping my fellow students grasp therapeutic concepts and paradigms. But to be honest, I just couldn't stomach the notion of therapy to help a person anymore. That rubbish had passed its sell-by-date. But the real nail in the coffin was having to endure an hour of personal development at the end of class to get in touch with our core self and develop our empathic skills both to ourselves and our class mates. It was painful. You can never go back after liberation: the show is over. One good thing, though — I never read it in a book. I saw it for myself.

The spontaneous recognition of Wholeness, timelessness and simple being — what I have referred to elsewhere as 'non-duality' — did what no therapy could ever have done: it got rid of *me*. All attempts at fixing and soul-searching just stop without permission. There is nothing there that needs changing or improving. Improvement is relevant only for the imposter who masquerades as an independent thing. That which appeared as a negotiator and peace maker for a pseudo self and a pseudo world dissolves. It is no longer needed. The search for special-ness under the guise of enlightenment is abandoned. The motivation, the drive for something better in the future, fuelled by a false sense of selfhood, splutters, chugs, hops and finally runs out of gas. You disembark from your vehicle and walk on your own. No more pulling levers or pressing pedals; there is only the self-propulsion of eternity itself.

There is nothing to work with anymore. Like a potter who has run out of clay; shaping fresh air becomes a silly and pointless exercise. At some level there is a recognition that the idealised self was like a vase with the wobbles on the potter's wheel; left like this and it becomes all contorted and twisted — ugly!

The World Is My Scapegoat

The title of this chapter could so easily have been the title of the book; the difference is that it would have been written in more negative terms. Scapegoating consists of placing blame on a person, group or organisation for some painful or unsatisfactory event and then casting them out into the wilderness to perish along with the problems and so restore normality or equilibrium.

The link with this book is that early painful and unsatisfactory encounters with people create an imaginary internal drama populated with heroes and villains. This remains unconscious but it impacts on us with anxiety, depression and feelings of worthlessness and longing. The heroes, villains and all the other characters become our world. However — and here is the astounding thing that the person or seeker will never even contemplate — the internal battle is dramatised and externalised. In fact dramatisation and externalisation, in the way I'm using them here, are synonymous.

Externalisation is an attempt to relieve the tension of Wholeness trying to depart from itself. It is now other people and social situations that are the problem and not the conflict brought about by the creation of selfhood and separation. Looked at in this way, the entire world is acting as a scapegoat upon which we can dump all the tension that the feeling of separateness creates.

To blame the world for not providing adequately for us, although it is painful and induces anxiety, seems far better than to realise that the edifice created to manage the world is no more powerful than *The Wizard of Oz*. The loss of an identity, any identity — even one that's clearly not coping and full of fear and misery — is met with the reality of annihilation. This is what hurts like hell when the truth rises and reclaims its homeland. I find this torment impossible to escape. Losing one's so-called life is the greatest loss there is.

This great 'loss' reveals an unchanging, unstructured aliveness that has always been here. It just *is*. It can't be analysed because it has no structure — in other words, it contains no parts or pieces. It is impossible to say what it is because it has no opposite. Saying what it is will be based on knowledge from the drama called 'me and my life'.

Blaming and scapegoating are deception. Take an honest look at yourself and ask if this is what you want. In my experience, which is all I have to offer, when the link with the past that is full of 'shoulds' and 'oughts' and future expectations is severed, you simply mature. You are no longer manipulated by inner dictates based on an impossible image of perfection constructed for psychic survival; you embrace spontaneity — in fact you *are* spontaneity.

Inner structures are no longer needed. They were only there to protect the pseudo sense of self. When that goes, the structures go. Structures are made from mental energy and always feel tight. When the mental energy that was once used for protection is used for enjoyment and exploration instead, there is simply relaxation.

This relaxation could be interpreted as being taken over by something — divine guidance or cosmic consciousness — but it's simply the stark contrast that comes into view. Nothing has been taken in or gained. It's like the removing of tight shoes scenario: you had forgotten what freedom for the feet felt like.

For me, all the studying, all the therapy and all the self-help books were of limited usefulness. The strange language of non-duality uprooted ignorance once and for all. There was no other tool that had the persistence or strength to do the job.

The thing with non-duality is that it has a life of its own. It'll throw you around anywhere it pleases. It will take you here; it will take you there. I was so highly structured inside with heroes and villains that any previous attempts at eliminating anxiety and self-doubt were about as effective as low-grade weed killer — they worked on the stem and left the root to produce more viable and live material in the future.

However, there is a curious thing that I have noticed regarding psychology books and theories of self and general human neuroses to which they alert us. When the separate self is seen to be false, there is an openness to appreciating theories of psychological development in greater depth than before. There doesn't seem to be a version of absolute perfection getting in the way that always used to discount what I would dismiss as the 'rubbish' of do-gooders.

I think I was just a tough nut to crack. When there is no me, it is realised there never was a me. Any pain, any suffering, all mental characters, in fact the entire drama of separation can be placed at the feet of Wholeness. Perverse? Maybe. Painful? Yes. A mistake? No!

Whatever it is that does everything, exhausts every single avenue of thought and explanation. When the mind comes up with an answer, it will be off again after a while, sniffing out elements of doubt to throw a spanner in the works and spoil everything you have toiled and worked hard for.

If you have a tough mind, you will go the distance right up to mental breakdown, serious illness or even the cessation of this functioning body. Thought will never outwit nature, though. Nature will always produce a tougher opponent that requires more and more of your mental energy to contain and control.

It seems Wholeness cannot accept that it is already perfect and complete. It tries to fool itself by appearing as things that seem different and separate. It feels the deception is watertight for many, many years and the deception is not questioned. Some lives appear to be very successful with good relationships, lots of money and a strong sense of self-worth. But these qualities you perceive in others are your own fantasies because you refuse to look at yourself. Envy and jealousy appear because your image of perfection is not the perfection of timelessness and Wholeness.

The world of form — from the perspective of the individual — is a world to be conquered and beaten into submission. A sense of control must be maintained to prolong the illusion, and enemies are created for the sake of self-righteousness.

If you have read George Orwell's *Nineteen Eighty-Four*, you may remember the frequent news updates delivered to the people regarding the progress of wars in far-off lands and the propaganda depicting 'others' as being enemies of the state and by association — Big Brother. Enemies created legitimacy and solidarity and staved off uncertainty. Limits and boundaries were created around thought, and if successful, thoughts were eventually controlled from within by a symbolic Big Brother whose eyes see everything.

Nineteen Eighty-Four may have been Orwell's attempt at hyperbole to shock us out of so-called normality and into reality; novelists of his calibre can speak to us if we have the capacity to decipher allegory. If not, then stories are simply entertaining — something to occupy the mind on a cold, dark, winter's night. Fiction, parables and spiritual texts can offer us a way out of the prison of separateness — but they do not spoonfeed us. You have been fed this way all your life from highchair to high school. It's time to mature, put on your battle gear and fight the dragon at the gates of the unknown. You may visit distant lands and face many trials and challenges. If you are lucky you will die and return victorious; unlucky, and you will fight for your life both at home and away for many a year to come.

This feeling of being alone and face to face with oneself is not negative; it is the opposite of conventionality. You've looked out into the world all your life searching for scapegoats that let you down, that should have cared for you in your hour of need. Parental figures and other institutions are symbolised internally and at the same time projected out to furnish an otherwise empty world. Some call this socialisation; I call it hypnotism.

Thinking for oneself and questioning reality is seldom undertaken. The hypnotic spell is strong. For me Orwell wasn't alerting us to the possible outcome of an untethered totalitarian regime — he was pointing to control mechanisms operating already, under the guise of normality and socialisation. Social engineering doesn't have to be overt as it is in *Nineteen Eighty-Four*: it can pass as conservatism or liberal ideology, if we are steered towards the right history books and the right so-called scholars. Ideologies can form identities and make strong sticks to beat the unenlightened into subservience and submission. We don't necessarily feel abused or beaten, we hold up our heads and say, 'I'm a Social Reformist' or, 'I'm a Liberal.' It's comforting to know who we are: it makes sense.

Fiction, literature and art often say more than the surface structure reveals. It is this hidden element in all spiritual texts and thought-provoking works that is worth finding, or more likely, stumbling upon.

Breath-taking Stuff!

If you are trying to get something from this book or any others attempting to describe the indescribable, nothing I have said so far will be much good. True, you might say to a fellow seeker, 'Have you read that new book by that Bates fellow, the locksmith? It's worth a look.' I guarantee it will soon be forgotten for the latest book from someone else or the latest YouTube incarnation. Seeking is a bit of a paradox because it means losing an identity, and this isn't always what people want. Seeking is comforting in a perverse way. However, when not finding is finding and not knowing is knowing, you will find and you will know. Unfortunately, the guy or girl who you thought would be ecstatic at the discovery has actually done a bunk. S/he has missed the fireworks, the ceremony, and the certificate. This is not a bad thing: s/he was a terrible drain on your resources anyway.

Good riddance!

Allegory and Storytelling

A Google search tells me that allegory is a literary device that uses narrative which appears normal and straightforward at first glance, only to be steeped in deeper meaning and social import if we look under the surface structure. You could place, I suppose, Jesus' parables as allegory. Think of the farmer sowing his seeds as spiritual teaching. Seeds that fall on various conditions are analogous to the hearing or rejection of the message: some seeds flourish and other remain dormant and unchanged by poor environmental conditions.

In a sense, all stories do this to some extent, even the text on the tube of children's toothpaste explaining the importance and supervision of caring for your child's little toothy pegs. It assumes the incompetence of a minor and positions you as a teacher to ensure a regular personal hygiene regime. In a subtle way, text found on something as innocuous as a tube of toothpaste sets up and reinforces patterns to guide us to life-saving skills and correct action.

But order and so-called knowledge have a knack of eroding the mystery and magic in life. It positions us in a social jigsaw puzzle to create a version of reality recognisable to ourselves, our friends, and also our enemies — we are given our script. A sense of order and belonging is a serious matter when we are young. Think of anyone from your school days who was a little different from the norm. There may have been differences in their dress sense, their body shape or father's profession. You will remember what a tough time they probably had. Was that you?

Stories, though, are not the problem. Believing them to be a final version of reality strangles creativity, fosters misery and depression and dampens down the flame of 'not knowing'. But I guess there is a kind of comfort in making sense of things: it aids in the predictability that characterises thought. Correctly identifying the shadow of a predator based on memory can leave you to fight another day and spread your genes around to ensure continuity as well as change.

Stories, I would say, are a device to point to something else: they point to timeless, immovable infinity and beingness. You appear as all your stories and all your scenes. You shape and contort yourself into infinite disguises. I love the original meaning of 'person'. Its root is 'persona' which refers to the mask actors wore on stage in antiquity. The 'sona' part of the word points to the mouth piece that projects the voice, the dialogue or song. Nowadays, the concept of a persona is more recognised as independence and separation.

We are all unique and each has a different story to tell and life to embellish. But uniqueness is not separate, underneath or inside anything. All stories are Wholeness and unchanging intimate Being. Timelessness and Wholeness are appearing as apparent time and apparent fragmentation. This is why life's jagged edge and irregular shapes are just as spiritual as cushion sitting and mantra chanting. Stillness and movement define each other.

I have just come back from the cinema with my son as these words are appearing, and whilst I was losing myself in *The Adventures of Tintin: The Secret of the Unicorn*. I also managed to look around at the cinema and at the audience who were spending their time in the same way I was. What I noticed is that the dots and dashes of the cinema screen that flashed on and off in rapid succession were the same sparkles that appeared in the form of other people sitting in the cinema house. One picture we take as fiction and make believe, while to the other one we give much more credibility. There isn't really any difference in the credibility. We get lost in both appearances. The difference we try to maintain is that we feel we walk away from the drama at the pictures and back to the daily grind of work, shopping and making ends meet. Both are fiction; both are fantasy.

True, we can't seem to dodge bullet after bullet and never get a bruise from a scuffle with a scoundrel, but notice the effortlessness of seeing, hearing, touching, tasting and smelling. Who the hell's doing all that? Where is it coming from? The same place the cinema picture I suggest — from a projector. In our case the mind performs this function, but unlike the cinema it never runs out of film: it gets threaded sideways, upside down and back to front on a continuous loop. The picture always looks different but the same pixels just change location from time to time.

The Message That Floats Your Boat

There's another unfathomable aspect of this. Why should a message that points to the same thing as a hundred other books and teachings strike a chord, and yet others do not? Is there a ripeness to hear? Have you crossed over the threshold and now walk where masters have walked? The simple answer is, I don't know. All I will say is that words both written and spoken, when put into certain combinations, seem to transmit something above and beyond the raw data. There is something that rings a bell. It might be the same book or the same dreary old meeting listening to question after question of the seeking mind that this time appears to uproot ignorance and everyday normality. You can hear yourself saying: 'Why didn't I see this before? How could I have missed something so obvious and simple?' That, I'm afraid, is not up for grabs. Wholeness sees when it sees and that's that. It pulls that veil so tight it's a wonder any light can get in at all.

For myself, I was so engrossed in my inadequate life and the attempts through therapy and psychology to fix the damn thing that considering This was not on the menu. When I met Lynn at the gym, even though she never overtly tried to change me in any way at all, something had started to shift and stir. Our conversations were normal and everyday generally, but a non-verbal, invisible to the naked eye resonance seemed to be operating. That's the best I can do, because to be honest, I don't know and I don't care. Forty odd years of timeless time had to occur before the spell lifted. It is a shame Rich was not able to see it. I guess it comes with the territory. Never mind, he was getting on my nerves anyway.

I have heard stories of people being drunk and disorderly spending another night slumped in a doorway somewhere with a guy pissing on their head for fun, with the vomit getting washed away with the stream of urine, and something is seen. They sober up, join a group and come back to life.

There is no book or satsang for this guy — that is far too tame and sensible. You wake when you wake and not before. That is why it is so frustrating at times I guess. But nothing needs to happen to be what you are. It is just that you only see that after awakening or at liberation. I told you this stuff sucks.

But maybe gobbledygook is better than perfect prose. Maybe the ordering and grammar of our sentences keeps us from 'the secret'. It makes me wonder if this is why poetry can touch us so deeply: it does not try and spell it out for us; we have to do some work with it and make it our own. We have so many chances to listen to others, whether live or from recordings. We create celebrities from our favourite speakers and get hooked on what they say. But like a weaning young animal, the mother gradually retreats to let the creature fend for himself, to explore for himself and to kill and destroy for himself. She may teach a few survival skills but the execution is all ours.

This message is not new; it doesn't belong just in the twenty-first century. Of course there is no twenty-first century, but if we enter into fantasy for a while, we can see that there have been many that have tried to transmit this message, some overtly and some covertly. Either way, you can see non-duality and Wholeness in texts stretching back for millennia. They are there for you to read when you've 'grown-up' somewhat and relinquished those ideas that were passed on in good faith and with little malice. When you see the trick and deception, there is no anger and resentment for what you have been through, though. There is just being, being, being.

Fantasy/Reality

Fantasy is what films are good at. Giant gorillas hanging from skyscrapers and Japanese plastic models stomping around screeching and wreaking havoc in our cities are great examples. We can enjoy this kind of thing and know where one world ends and another begins.

We tend to treat the ideas, beliefs and hypotheses the mind manufactures as faithful representations of what is actually happening out there in the real world of jobs, families and all human relationships. We certainly do not give the cinema screen activity the same credence as our own analyses and opinions. We base our judgments on a rationality and logic that are the hallmark of sanity and credibility in the world that is presented to us from the teachings we grew up with. We are certain we see what we see, and if someone else cannot see this obviousness, we can become silent, get angry, attack, and even kill to get our point across. We are so close to the thought that we believe it and create an identity out of a system that has worked once or twice in the past when the wind was blowing in the right direction and the crows were nesting high.

Thought and belief do enable us to function in this world of appearances and dramatic nuance and, to be fair, we manage quite well. Deals are struck and people do relax in each other's company. People marry and arguments do not last forever. Fantasy is amusing at times and allows some freezing over of consensus reality. It is fun to imagine an obnoxious and grumpy old boss sitting on the toilet with his trousers around his ankles to regain the certitude that human beings are all born equal, in some respects at least. In fact fantasy can be creative and illuminating; Albert Einstein said that the gift of fantasy meant more to him than his talent for absorbing knowledge.

But if we want to place fantasy above reality or reality above fantasy, it becomes troublesome and complex. Where is the benchmark and who decides? If I say I am walking into town to buy a loaf of bread, I am actually creating row after row of imaginary objects that I have labelled as real and out there. Yes, there seems to be a loaf of bread in my hand and not a shotgun, but this labelling is very restrictive and uncomfortable. A loaf of bread has many ingredients and has appeared through process and activity. Language can imprison the user and the appearance, close off channels of mystery and awe, and package the world for consumption in the future. Everything that appears to happen is simply arising out of nothing and nowhere. There is only this, only Wholeness, which can appear as anything, even loaves of bread. You cannot grasp or capture time and place because they are not here. Fantasy creates a sense of permanence the same way the model maker or make-up artist creates a monster to terrorise a neighbourhood or rampage through a school.

Fantasy in the guise of permanence allows you to leave your house in the morning and talk to your work colleagues about how dreadfully the builders are converting your attic. Language enables words to stand for apparent existing entities. Words and phrases like 'shoddy workmanship' or 'flooded kitchen' stand in for what you believe to be real tangible things or entities in the world. But if you are at your desk drinking your coffee and chatting to Betty in accounts, then that is reality. Your builders, your house and flooded kitchen are non-existent. You could pop home, I suppose, in your lunch break to confirm you are not imagining things, but you would still only see the contents of your own mind projected out to replicate the calamity this morning.

This is so difficult to write and to convey because it brings crashing down the cornerstone you call reality. Few of us question the legitimacy of objects and events; it's just the way it is. We will still pay for the work when it's finished or throw our builders off site when we get home and look for another to finish the job. What is being suggested is that the process of abstraction, storytelling and hypnotism creates this magical, wonderful life of appearances that entertain and allow no-thing to appear as all this incredible array of things and dramas. All events, whether it's watching a birth, mending your bike or cooking the dinner, are all the same — Wholeness, being and inseparability.

You have always been here, you were not born at some time and some place. You will not die because you were not born. You have always been the timeless, dressed in purpose, meaning and journey. What a load is shrugged off when the dream is rumbled and seen for what it is. Fifty foot gorillas are reduced to children's action figures. Children's action figures are up there with angels and miracles.

Fantasy and reality, like everything else, define each other and do not exist apart. There is only this—forever and ever and ever. Nothing is moving and nothing is changing. Permanence, stability and reality can never be seen or experienced. They don't need to be. Thinking that you are experiencing something familiar and everyday is the stuff of dreams. Wholeness likes to dream; it is good drama, good entertainment. Deep sleep must get boring after a while—not much going on. A good old dream wakes us up when we sleep and when we think we are separate and alone. Appearance is dream, every last bit of it. It appears as awareness and in awareness. Consciousness never comes and never goes. It is infinite, timeless and unfathomable.

Thank the lord!

Come Fly with Me

I have mentioned 'space' a few times in the course of these words you are reading and assume you know what it is I am talking about. Generally speaking, it is considered to be that in which our villages, towns and cities exist. It is reaching through something in order to grasp an object and bring it closer to examine or consume in some way. Objects seem to take up space and so there is a limit to how many tiny objects you could fit in a match box or how much refuse and rubble a skip or dumpster will hold when improving the house or garden.

Space is what we travel through to get somewhere. A trip to the United States or Africa appears to take time and follow a course that can be verified by a map that someone else has drawn based on similar journeys taken in the past. This is fine as far as it goes. I mean, a trip to the States for me will take many hours from Heathrow or Gatwick in the UK, and so I will be packing my iPod to entertain me and not be content with the safety instructions in the pouch in front of me on the plane.

But spend a bit of time and examine a little closer. Space is experience. There is a knowing and feeling associated with it. The office I am in at the moment is about 3 metres by 3 metres, in everyday language, and feels pretty compact and bijou. Las Vegas, on the other hand, was a mighty big place when I visited, with structures that dwarfed just about everything in my little corner of the globe. My office is small; Las Vegas is big.

This distinction is bogus. Let me explain. I am looking at my cream-painted wall in front of me as I am typing and, to be honest, it could do with a spot of touching up or redecoration here and there. I can see bits of paint missing from sticky tape and the odd Blu-Tack mark. There seems to be a pattern if I use my imagination: the missing paint patches are little towns in the distance and the ripple textures from the paint roller are rolling fields punctuated by a few sheep and cows grazing on the grass before me. There is a pattern of light and it's seducing my imagination to make up stories of 'out there' and separate.

Whether I am being amazed at the bright lights of Vegas or the splodges and imperfections of my office wall, fantasy is weaving its magic to make something out of nothing. I cannot have space separate from 'me' because when 'Vegas' or my office appears, so do I. I am labelling experience to be something in particular. So I am convincing myself that one pattern of light is called Las Vegas and another pattern my scruffy office wall, or, 'country scene'. They are both experience and I am not separate from that. Las Vegas is abstraction both when I am talking about my trip to a place in Nevada and also when I think I am actually located somewhere very bright and in your face on Planet Earth. Thought is constantly editing to create the illusion that we are in our bag of skin and something permanent and separate is outside of us, with an independent existence. We only need enough so-called people to play along with us and we have got a real good game going on.

If you are puzzled by this, think of a dream. Whilst dreaming, common-sense tells us we are lying down somewhere, usually in a bed, and a world is appearing full of people, places and objects. There appears to be space full of most things you would find on Earth. There seems to be depth in the dream, so the dream body seems to be able to traverse the world in much the same way you do on waking up. No matter what goes on in a dream, on waking it does not take long to realise it was all imagined. Thought was up to its old tricks again and you appeared lost for a while in ideas and memory. Forget, for a moment, the interpretation of dreams as trying to tell you something profound about the inner workings of your psyche. A dream is much more than that. A dream is screaming at you to wake up and see it for what it is. It seems we can do this fine in the cool light of day when the 'normal' returns, such as not being able to fly or realising that monsters belong in story books and film. We seem to be able to accept space and time as illusory in our dreams, but do not allow this formulation in the waking state.

There is a common denominator to the dream state and the waking state, and that is knowing or experiencing. There is no such thing as space without experiencing. If you have ever experienced so called 'space' and been absent, I would like you to write a book about it and convince me. My imagination is pretty good, but that one is surely a mindbender to end all mindbenders. Mathematicians and physicists may be able to establish the reality of space using formulas and equations. Not bad. But equations in the head or written down for public scrutiny are just more experiencing. Give up. You cannot win.

Places, people, buildings and mountains are made from thought and not matter. Matter is another word for experiencing and not separate from it. How fantastic this all is, how breath-taking! Armed with this, you would not believe the sigh of relief from Wholeness. It is the same sigh of relief when you realise you have not lost your holiday money in a dream game of cards, nor has your arm been amputated in a dream car crash. Nothing that appears is real. What is real does not appear, ever. You will never find it. If you think you have, then write a book about that as well. I wouldn't mind taking a peek at the manuscript first, though: I am always looking for something to get the barbecue going. If you are smart and full of charm and charisma, I am sure you will accumulate a following of some sort after you have put pen to paper. Count me out though. The only thing I follow is my nose to a good bar for a fine pint of ale or a good Indian restaurant for a good curry.

Sorry.

Children: No Better Guru

I just have to put finger to keyboard: I am sitting in my office looking out the window in the wake of a stormy night. I can see a little girl, no more than three-years-old, standing on the kerb in bright pink wellies gazing into the puddle below. Her mum seems to be goading her to have a splash. Without any further encouragement, in she goes. Back on the kerb and the bravery increases: 'One, two, five—jump' I imagine she is saying. Not one penny was needed to simply enjoy one of nature's treasures. Not only that, her mum's face was beaming as well, enjoying the entertainment from the safety of dry land.

I am mesmerised momentarily and stop in my tracks. For that small sample of time, the girl was not just simply playing in the water; she *was* the water. I bet there was no worrying about getting her trousers wet or considering mum having to wash them. No thinking, *I had better be sensible because mum has got enough to do with the dinner to cook and the mountain of ironing to scale.* She was simply being.

This is what never really leaves us: the joy of just being. It might get covered or buried to a great depth, but when Wholeness stops pretending to be a thing that can be described, it greets itself like the prodigal son returning to the embrace of the father. It was a journey that had to be made because the joy of the return cannot be felt without some time in the wilderness. There is no mistake. It is what it is.

Children can teach us so much more than any book or master can do. They represent unconditional love in a tangible non-abstract way. Just watch any two or three-year-old playing: it sends shivers up your spine if you look without seeing and understand without thinking. They have not chosen to play: playing happens. They have not chosen to cry; they are simply crying. Conditioning and adult sensibilities, although inevitable and part of the play of being human, play a major part in hiding what is plain to see and withholding what you can easily grasp. I am not being negative here; in fact I celebrate conditioning now. How else can you see through bullshit without creating a piece to sample?

If you are spellbound by the drama of living and want to feel you are a responsible parent, you will want your child to be similar to other children and eventually similar to, or possibly more successful than, yourself. Gradually, we are taught how to see and how to think. Education slims us down so we can fit into any niche available. This simplifies things, and so homogeneity seems easier to document and deliver than heterogeneity. We can write our ten-yearly Census for the ones that take our place.

I mentioned the socially constructed self and how some theorists do not talk about Freudian structures that reside within; rather they emphasise emergent selves through activity and discourse. Looked at in this way, we find eighteenth, nineteenth or twenty-first century personalities. There are no immortal souls that will find their way to heaven aboard the 'good person' express. Ideas about who we are and what life means change with our sentences and our sciences.

There is little attempt within this paradigm to impose natural structure on the social world. The self is always seen as an historical artefact that has an ad hoc nature to it. Ideas and beliefs shape, and are shaped by, human sensibilities. It seems then that the isolated individual thinking his thoughts and having a secluded inner life with purpose and intention is a cultural and changeable phenomenon. The old hypnotise the young through language and an appeal to historical progress. That is what is on offer; that is what you have to work with.

This is why splashing in a puddle or playing in a sand-pit are transcendental. There is no sense of end-gaining from these activities or getting it right. You cannot make mistakes playing, or become confused about the details in a rule book about puddle splashing or sandcastle making.

There is no better grasping of what we mean by time-lessness than being with children and letting them show us how to let go and just be. There seems to be very little of that censoring and self-consciousness for the child that can easily plague an adult who feels the stage lights and critical audience when new activities — and old, for that matter — are embarked upon. The gradual building up of an identity through our early adventures and mis-adventures and throughout life provides predictability and a knowledge base that sets a pattern for all future behaviour. Spontaneity has grown guidelines — what a contradiction in terms!

If you have a feeling for what I am trying to describe — you might have smiled at the description of the little girl puddle splashing earlier on — then you have already been where the girl is now. I do not need to go into any further detail to get my point across. You know. It has never gone away. Timelessness has dressed itself up. It has been in drag. You have become lost in the imagination of growing-up and growing old. You thought you had a purpose, a job, a spouse and a duty to perform. You are dreaming about the non-existent, the past, the future and the now. The unceasing sparkles of life have become like daggers, poking and piercing, prodding and provoking.

Liberation is letting go of the seriousness of the story — not the story itself. The world is staggering. Just look around and feel it. Ask yourself what is going on and reject with the utmost conviction any answer that pops into your head. Life has no answer. It just *is*. Children know this but cannot say; animals know this but do not care. Adults *think* they know this and that is the problem.

When you are immersed in the drama of life it is impossible to accept that there is nothing wrong with anything. You will provide data from wars, famine and homeless people. You will look at the disabled and the poor and bang your fists down, demanding a reason for all this mess. You will hope that Hitler has gone to hell and Mother Teresa to heaven. But engineering a peace process and feeding the starving is an activity that simply occurs or not. You don't do it. It happens. Likewise, pulling over whilst driving to help a stranded motorist is a kind thing to do: the steering wheel goes left rather than straight on, and two wheels mount the pavement to enquire about assistance. Just like playing is for the child, life does it all. You are off the hook.

Hatch, Match and Dispatch

Open up your local newspaper and you will probably find a page with births, marriages and deaths. Laid before you is all of life, wrapped up in print like a portion of fish and chips. Familiar names may grab your attention and thoughts like, *Ooh, they've had a baby*, or, *Wow, they finally got hitched. That won't last!* Or finally, *Arrh, shame... he used to be a bloody good darts player as well.*

We are experiencing emotions in the same manner as if we are turning the pages of our favourite novel. Both are embellished; both are fictitious. We can cry with our novels and cry when we experience loss, joy and anger. We do not manufacture these emotions—they simply arise. Have you ever tried to stop yourself crying to avoid embarrassment when you are with others, or had the giggles when you are supposed to be serious? It is a battle, isn't it? Emotions are so overwhelming; you cannot separate yourself from them. In that moment your identity is the emotion; you are not a person experiencing them.

This is more about death than relationships and birth. Death is a real conundrum, more so than birth or marriage. Where will we go? What will it be like? Will we be punished? Who else will be there? Will we find out the secret?

We could go on and on with this list and I am sure you can provide your own ideas and fears. More than anything else, non-being and nothingness cannot be sorted out using logic and reasoning. No one has come back from the dead and told us what to expect. Sure there is documentation for near-death experiences. But near-death is not death. Whatever it is, someone comes back and tell us what they experienced — light, tunnels and peace. These are experiences; they are known. Death is surely absence of the one that knows. If it's known... you are not dead, are you?

Deep sleep is surely a kind of death. There is an absence here as well, but any notion of absence is a concept like anything else. We talk about it whilst thought is operating and not in conversation between two dead people. So, this is what makes death a no brainer. You would think logic of this nature would quieten the mind. In actuality it appears to stimulate it. It can go off on one and start religions and faiths to account for supernatural activity. The mind does not let logic get in the way of a good scary story. It will conjure up and pull no end of rabbits out the hat. It is its job, you see. It cannot help it. It has to know something. Knowing nothing is not an option. That is fine and dandy. Leave it alone. You will only make it worse if you seem interested.

Perhaps death is all there is. Apparent life is death at room temperature. A little cooler is dream stuff and fantasy. Look at it as you will. Death will always be clothed in fantasy like everything else experienced. This does not mean we laugh and joke when a loved one goes still and stiff and stops talking. Powerful emotions arise and show themselves, and memories occupy our thoughts more than listening to the words of condolence our friends and relatives offer. We grieve.

My dad died in 2002 from mesothelioma, a cancer caused by exposure to asbestos on building sites in the '60s and early '70s. I remember touching his cold, hard body and thinking he felt like a shop dummy. We could not talk not even to argue. There he was, no more than 70 pounds of skin and bone occupying only half of a single bed. What got to me was watching the funeral directors carrying him downstairs in a black body bag. It reminded me of a butcher with a pig slung over his shoulder. Both had ceased to be; only we whisk our corpses away from the gaze of the living. It's hushed up, this dying lark.

Surprisingly, this first experience of death of someone close had more than one emotion or thought attached. Yes, there was sadness and a sense of loss, but there was also a knowing at some level that there is only life. Death is not the end of anything. If it is the end, then what was it that began? My dad never manufactured his birth or death. The processes that form the body are the same ones that eventually clear it away. Everything is taken care of.

The bizarre notion that you, the person, must surely continue somewhere is a hellish idea. Nothingness is actually what we crave for. It is what we want. It is what we are. A good old eventful 'life' with troubles, fears and frustrations and feeling lost and alone allows Wholeness to eventually see itself in all its glory. The sheer power gets released and explodes with the ferocity of a million earthquakes. The dream finally ends never to return. Ah, peace at last!

Now do not get all stupid and make sense of any of that. The peace you crave is already here; it is in the sound of a crying baby and the screech of Godzilla. The song *There's No Place Like Home* is quite right. Home has no place at all, no edge and no boundary. Home you carry within and without. You are always at home attending to the affairs of today. Keep your house in order if you wish and plump up those cushions. You never know, an old friend might pop in. You have to be ready.

The Tentacles of the Universe

Newton's calculations from the late seventeenth and early eighteenth century enabled human beings to negotiate space with the same precision it built its skyscrapers and made its sports cars. Perfect. With the moon landings in the 1960's science came up trumps once again.

Science has got a habit of being a bit sneaky, though, and economical with the truth. I am not going to enter into conspiracy theories that question the moon landings; I am questioning who the hell went to the moon. On the one hand, the physicists tell us the universe consists of atoms and stuff, and this stuff was manufactured in stars eons ago. In the next breath, they talk of human advancement and more accurate predictions. If the universe is essentially energy, then Planet Earth that appears as humans and everything else is stretching out its tentacles and having a good feel of itself. Fantasy tells another story. Fantasy creates evolution and advancement. Fantasy creates division.

The spacecraft, the shuttle, the occupants—all are made from the same stuff as the moon. There is no separate something observing something else that is alien. It is all one. Always has been, always will be. The big bang is not some event that happened long ago and created all this.

The big bang never went away: it has just cooled down a bit and looks like this now. I have heard it described as like throwing a bottle of ink against a wall and observing the vast array of twirling patterns at the periphery. The patterns are Wholeness patterning, appearing as space exploration and technological advancement.

All there is, can only ever experience itself; it never experiences objects. Objects or appearances reflect Wholeness because experiencing comes with 'objects' and objects come with experiencing. It is so obvious when seen and so hidden when looked for. Experience can appear as full moons, half-moons, crescent moons and cratered moons. It can be sampled by hand and sampled by sight. There is no definitive thing called 'moon'. Moon is an abstraction used for communication purposes. The moon stretches out its own tentacles back to Earth in the form of oceanic movement we call tides. There is no such thing as one-way traffic.

I enjoy science and marvel at what appears to be. But no matter how sophisticated we have become, it all goes 'puff' in deep sleep. No computers or progress here. There's just timelessness having a rest for a bit, ready for more mayhem tomorrow. If someone gave you a lethal injection whilst asleep, you wouldn't care less, would you? Have the same attitude now. The universe won't mind.

The Relief

Like the tight shoes scenario described earlier, seen in this way, a sense of peace ensues. Not the kind of peace when the spouse and kids are out for a while so you could make love to your iPod for an hour or so, whilst sipping a beer. That is very nice; I have done that more than once. No, the peace I am referring to is the one that is here in a busy shop, in a dentist's chair or listening to a road drill outside your bedroom window. It is more like acceptance of what is rather than this constant pushing and pulling at life. In this peace, there seems to be the time to do things at whatever pace you feel like. There is a noticing of what is going on right now rather than constant thoughts about what next. An earthworm or an ants' nest grabs your attention and there is just looking without trying to describe what is happening. There is no separation between the one who is looking and what is looked at.

The facial muscles relax and the wrinkled brow flattens out. Something has been released from its imprisonment and is enjoying the freedom. There is a realisation that you tied your own hands together and fastened the straps to the straitjacket. It has all been a game. No need to stop playing though; games are fun. Even better when they are felt as real and out there. Imagination has an enormous power when believed in. But it's like going to the cinema, you have to forget the camera man, the lighting crew and the editor's skill — that would spoil the enjoyment. This is what Wholeness does: it loses itself in the drama of its own creation. It pretends to be a separate thing existing in time and space with a limited lifespan. It cannot be any different; losing is finding I suppose. It kind of makes the return home something special. The battles and the victories in great literature from the Odyssey to Moby Dick mirror the war within you.

So, no need to call this a spiritual book; that sounds too fancy. Think of it like when your parents or whoever tell you about the facts of life — you know, where babies come from. The myth you carried around in your head gets shattered and something else, a bit strange and a bit messy, takes its place. It turns out the truth is stranger than anything you concocted yourself. It just takes a while to accept it and incorporate it into your life.

But like the mirror analogy for the title of this book — reflect on it!

CONSCIOUS.TV is a TV channel which broadcasts on the internet at www.conscious.tv. It also has programmes shown on several satellite and cable channels around the world. The channel aims to stimulate debate, question, enquire, inform, enlighten, encourage and inspire people in the areas of Consciousness, Non-Duality and Science. It also has a section called 'Life Stories' with many fascinating interviews.

There are over 200 interviews to watch including several with communicators on Non-Duality including Jeff Foster, Steve Ford, Suzanne Foxton, Gangaji, Greg Goode, Scott Kiloby, Richard Lang, Francis Lucille, Roger Linden, Wayne Liquorman, Jac O'Keefe, Mooji, Catherine Noyce, Tony Parsons, Satyananda, Richard Sylvester, Rupert Spira, Florian Schlosser, Mandi Solk and Pamela Wilson. There is also an interview with UG Krishnamurti.

Do check out the channel as we are interested in your feedback and any ideas you may have for future programmes. Email us at info@conscious.tv with your ideas or if you would like to be on our email newsletter list.

CONSCIOUS.TV and NON-DUALITY PRESS
present two unique DVD *releases*

CONVERSATIONS ON NON-DUALITY – VOLUME 1
Tony Parsons – The Open Secret • Rupert Spira –
The Transparency of Things – Parts 1 & 2 • Richard
Lang – Seeing Who You Really Are

CONVERSATIONS ON NON-DUALITY – VOLUME 2
Jeff Foster – Life Without a Centre • Richard
Sylvester – I Hope You Die Soon • Roger Linden –
The Elusive Obvious

Available to order from: www.non-dualitypress.org

New Book now available to order from NON-DUALITY PRESS

CONVERSATIONS ON NON-DUALITY
Twenty-Six Awakenings

The book explores the nature of true happiness, awakening, enlightenment and the 'Self' to be realised.

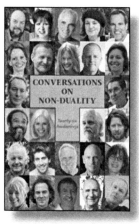

It features 26 expressions of liberation, each shaped by different life experiences and offering a unique perspective.

The collection explores the different ways 'liberation' happened and 'suffering' ended. Some started with therapy, self-help workshops or read books written by spiritual masters, while others travelled to exotic places and studied with gurus. Others leapt from the despair of addiction to drugs and alcohol to simply waking up unexpectedly to a new reality.

The 26 interviews included in the book are with: David Bingham, Daniel Brown, Sundance Burke, Katie Davis, Peter Fenner, Steve Ford, Jeff Foster, Suzanne Foxton, Gagaji, Richard Lang, Roger Linden, Wayne Liquorman, Francis Lucille, Mooji, Catherine Noyce, Jac O'Keeffe, Tony Parsons, Bernie Prior, Halina Pytlasinska, Genpo Roshi, Florian Schlosser, Mandi Solk, Rupert Spira, James Swartz, Richard Sylvester and Pamela Wilson.

Lightning Source UK Ltd.
Milton Keynes UK
UKOW051818110213

206130UK00001B/15/P